# Profiles from History

## Leaders Who Changed Worlds Both Large and Small

### - Volume 3 -

## Ashley M. Wiggers

Profiles from History - Volume 3
Copyright © 2011 Ashley M. Wiggers

Portrait illustrations © 2011 Cheryl Ellicott
Map illustrations by Bryan Kummer

ISBN: 978-1-931397-71-1
Library of Congress Control Number: 2010916510

Published by Geography Matters, Inc.
800.426.4650
www.geomatters.com

Printed in the United States of America

# Dedication

*"Those who stand for nothing fall for anything."*

\- Alexander Hamilton

This book is dedicated to the reader.
May these stories of courage touch your heart, as they have mine.

Dad - Thank you for so faithfully encouraging and molding the writer in me.
I can only hope to someday be the kind of person and writer that you are.

# Table of Contents

# Instructions

In *Profiles from History - Volume 3*, I took a unique perspective on each historical figure by sharing some of the lesser known facts you may not have learned before. I have also included some people whose stories you may not have heard, but they certainly deserve our admiration. People like Irena Sendler and Dr. Charles Drew, who saved many lives with their determination and character. As you read each profile it is my hope that you will connect with the person, not just the history.

In this book you will read about authors, inventors, statesmen, everyday people, and war heroes that made a significant difference in the world around them and forever changed the future. Beginning around 1750 and continuing through 1950, the exploits of many famous people are described with an eye to seeing their motivations and the impact their lives had on others.

Use *Profiles from History* either to enhance lessons in history and social studies or as a stand-alone book. Choose the fun projects in this book according to the interests of each student. Select as many or as few of the activities as you would like. Each profile can be used as a read-aloud, or your student can use the story for independent reading. To get the full benefit from each profile, I recommend students use several of the following activities:

*Discussion questions:* inspire critical thinking and help the student relate to each historical figure.

*Follow-up activities:* relate to the accomplishments of each profile, connecting the child by hearing, seeing, and doing to the importance of each person's story.

*Word games:* such as word searches and crossword puzzles focus on key words to remember from the profile, increasing comprehension and retention of vocabulary.

*Critical thinking activities:* include activities such as creating their own true and false statements and determining the meaning of words using context.

*Maps:* help students visually pinpoint either the location where the historical figure came from, or the area in which a main event of their life took place.

*Timelines:* give students an overview of the time in which the historical figure lived and connects each person with other important events occurring at the same time. A reference timeline is included with each profile. Students are instructed to place timeline figures on a timeline along with two events that occurred during the life of the person studied. This timeline and the figures are located in the back of the book before the answer keys. Simply cut out each figure and place it on the timeline in the correct location. Tape the top edge of the figure only, that way the figure can be lifted to reveal the two extra events that the students wrote.

## Also Available

*Profiles from History - Volume 3* activities and reproducibles in digital format for your convenience.

If you enjoy the format and focus of this book you may also be interested in:

*Profiles from History - Volume 1* which includes profiles of men and women of great influence around the time of exploration and founding of our country, from the years 1200 -1890.

*Profiles from History - Volume 2* which mainly focuses on the heroes of American history during the Revolutionary and Civil Wars.

# Amos Fortune

Amos Fortune had every right to be bitter. He was taken from his home at the young age of about fifteen. Stolen from Africa where he was a free man, and taken to America, he was sold as a slave. His life was changed forever by the greedy ambitions of slave traders. Amos would never again be able to see his home, and it would be many years before he could enjoy the freedom that he had been born into.

Amos made the long journey to America, called the Middle Passage, around 1725. It's unimaginable to think of what he must have gone through. Slave ships used every bit of space possible to cram in people. The decks where they held the slaves were usually about three and a half feet high with no space to stand or stretch. Ships such as these often had many problems with disease because of the harsh environment.

Amos Fortune was fortunate, in that he ended up in the New England area. Many people were not so lucky. If you were sold in the West Indies, for example, you would be faced with an extremely rough life. He was also fortunate not to be taken to the other end of the U.S. where slaves were put to work in the fields of the south. Instead, Amos was brought to New England where slaves worked alongside their owners, learning their trade, or helping to care for a small farm. Since there were no large plantations like in the south, the need for owning slaves was less great. Because of this, only about 5% of the population in the north was black in the 18th century.

Amos spent about forty-five years of his life in slavery. Though his life was not his own, the men that purchased him treated him fairly well. Records show that Amos, though he never attended school, could read and write. It's possible that he was taught by Quakers who used to hold classes for Africans. There are no records of which port Amos arrived at or who he was first sold to. No one even knows exactly how he got his name. The first record of Amos Fortune is in the will of his then owner, Ichabod Richardson. Ichabod was a tanner (a person who converts the hides of animals into leather) who resided in Woburn, Massachusetts. In his will, Richardson stated that six years following his death Amos Fortune was to be set free. In another event that could have caused Amos to become bitter about his life, or give up on the idea of freedom, his master signed a new will just five days before his unexpected death. It mentioned nothing of Amos Fortune's freedom. At the time of Richardson's death, Amos was already 58 years old. I imagine that he must have felt as though life, with its cruel unfairness, had forgotten about him again.

But hope was just around the corner. Ichabod Richardson's heir drafted a document that required Amos to pay a certain amount of money and then receive his freedom. Amos made the last payment in 1770, when he was sixty years old.

Not much is known about him for the next few years. He bought half an acre of land in Woburn, on which he built a small house. During his life, Amos purchased the freedom of three different people. The first was an unnamed woman who sadly died soon after. The next was three years later, a woman named Lydia Somerset, whom he then married. She too died suddenly just three months after their marriage. Then there was Violate Baldwin. Her master's wife was Ichabod Richardson's first cousin, who attended the same church as the Richardsons. Amos and Violate might have met at the church in a section that was designated for Africans. Amos purchased Violate's freedom in 1778, when she was fifty years old. The two were married the next day.

In 1781, Amos and Violate moved from the place of their slavery to the town of Jaffrey, New Hampshire. While there, Amos opened a tannery. He soon became known as one of the best tanners in the region. Receipts show that people sent their business many miles to Amos. He bought twenty-five acres of land in Jaffrey, on which he built a small house and barn. Both are still standing today. The road to his house is now known as Amos Fortune Road. He was a devoted member of the local church and was instrumental in founding the first library in Jaffrey.

At the age of 91, Amos Fortune died. One year later, Violate followed her husband. Both are buried side by side in the town of Jaffrey. The following words were written as their epitaphs:

> *"Sacred to the memory of Amos Fortune, who was born free in Africa, a slave in America, he purchased liberty, professed Christianity, lived reputably, and died hopefully"*

> *"Sacred to the memory of Violate, by sale the slave of Amos Fortune, by marriage his wife, by her fidelity, his friend and solace, she died his widow"*

In his will, Amos designated that a "handsome present" be left to the church. He also left money in support of their local schoolhouse. His story became well known in 1950 when Elizabeth Yates wrote a children's book about his life named *Amos Fortune, Free Man*. It is a Newbery award-winning book that has been translated into several different languages, and continues to be taught about and read throughout the world.

There's something very noble about simply living your life the best way that you can. You might think that since Amos Fortune is in this book, he was possibly an inventor, or maybe became someone famous in his day. The truth is, he is only famous for the way in which he lived. Amos Fortune truly overcame adversity. He built a life of respect and honor for himself, and even in his death, his story continues to inspire anyone who hears it.

## Discussion

Amos Fortune's life seems very unfair. He was born free, and then captured into slavery for about half of his life. He lived the rest of his days as a respected citizen in the town of Jaffrey, New Hampshire, and purchased the freedom of others who had the same misfortune. He wouldn't let bitterness keep him from living a full life. Is there anything in your life that you could be bitter about? Talk with your parent about how you can choose not to be bitter like Amos when life seems unfair.

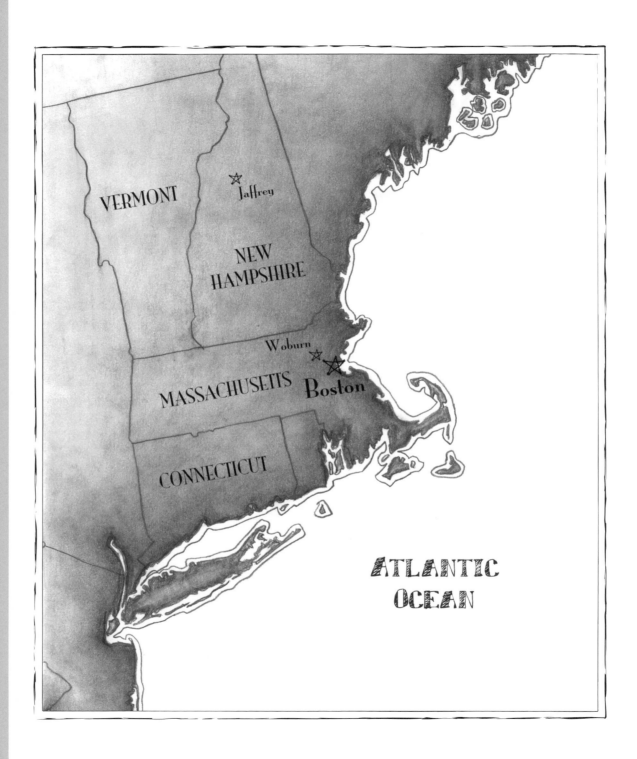

## Timeline Activity

Put things in perspective. Place Amos Fortune's figure on the timeline in the year 1770, which was when he purchased his freedom. Then identify two other events that happened in history during his life and add them to your timeline. You might also add a symbol or picture that represents this event.

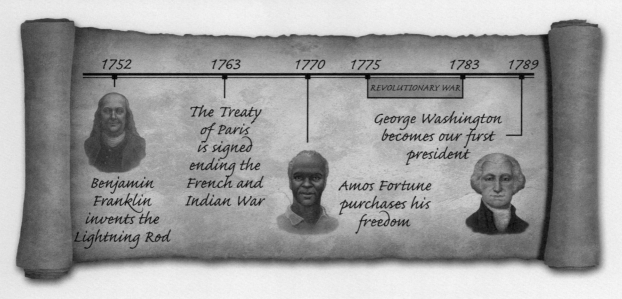

1752  1763  1770  1775  1783  1789

REVOLUTIONARY WAR

Benjamin Franklin invents the Lightning Rod

The Treaty of Paris is signed ending the French and Indian War

Amos Fortune purchases his freedom

George Washington becomes our first president

## Activity

Amos Fortune was an expert tanner. Tanners used many processes to create fine leather. Learn more about the different types of leather. What things are usually made of leather? Do you or your family members have anything made of leather? What are the benefits of having something made of leather? Do you think leather is as valuable as it used to be? Tell why you think it is or isn't.

## True or False

Create five true or false statements about this story. Present them to your family members. Mix up the true and false statements to keep everyone thinking. Be sure sure to make up an answer key so that your readers will know when they are correct. To see a sample True or False, turn to page 203.

## Wordscramble

Here is a list of scrambled words that relate to the profile you read about Amos Fortune. Unscramble the letters and write the words correctly.

1. rcAfai _____

2. ldBtVaiowinel _____

3. aIbadosdccRrinhho _____

4. aetrnn _____

5. bouWnr _____

6. umtonFeorAs _____

7. aryffJe _____

8. phaetpi _____

9. EzbeheiYlastta _____

10. meferod _____

## Using Context

Read the sentence and then look at the word in *italics*. Tell what you think that word means. Then look it up in a dictionary to confirm, or make sure of, the meaning. Tell someone about each word that you got correct. Remember, you will get better at understanding word meanings as you practice using context, or the words around a word.

1. His life was changed forever by the greedy *ambitions* of slave traders. (paragraph 1)

   I think *ambitions* means: _____

   Dictionary definition: _____

   My meaning was: (Circle one)    correct    had correct parts    not close

2. He was a devoted member of the local church and was *instrumental* in founding the first library in Jaffrey. (paragraph 7)

   I think *instrumental* means: _____

   Dictionary definition: _____

   My meaning was: (Circle one)    correct    had correct parts    not close

3. Amos Fortune truly overcame *adversity*. (paragraph 12)

   I think *adversity* means: _____

   Dictionary definition: _____

   My meaning was: (Circle one)    correct    had correct parts    not close

# Amos Fortune Word Search

```
N O S D R A H C I R D O B A H C I M E
K Q A I H K N Z T G Z C N C S F K O L
B S P M I V G Y W S N Z A V B U U D I
T M V I O L E T B A L D W I N M P E Z
A Y O O N S L Z L I Q H T F M E D E A
C Z N W B D F V T H Q I S L P P B R B
I X W R W J V O G T P F A A Q V C F E
R N F F U W T F R Z D A P T I J T D T
F T A D M B C H A T U P T H E A U P H
A J Y U I G O Z D L U V E I S W E O Y
K D N Y B V V W T V O N W W P F N V A
G A L G W V O X C W K I E F G E K J T
Y T W Q E T H W G M A I M S D C A G E
T E J T A N N E R T R J T F A Z T U S
V R V C Y S W I Y E R F F A J A S E H
```

## Word Bank

Africa

Amos Fortune

Elizabeth Yates

epitaph

freedom

Ichabod Richardson

Jaffrey

tanner

Violet Baldwin

Woburn

# Amos Fortune Crossword

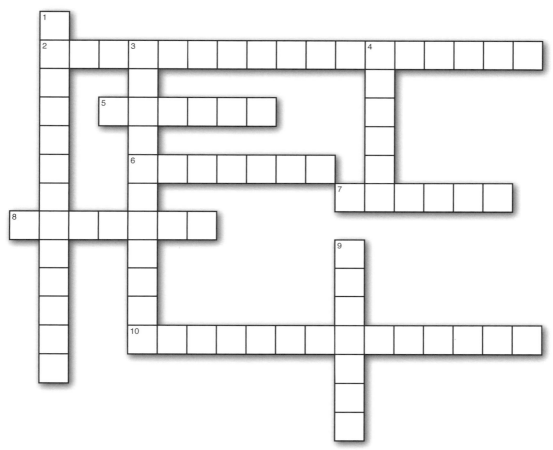

**Across**

2. man who taught Amos Fortune his trade
5. the Massachusetts city where Amos Fortune lived
6. the state of having no ties of obligation or bondage to others
7. someone who tans hides
8. final resting place of Amos Fortune
10. author of the famous book *Amos Fortune, Free Man*

**Down**

1. Amos Fortune's wife at the time of his death
3. man brought from Africa to America to be a slave
4. second largest continent
9. a phrase written in memory of a person

# George Washington

George Washington lived his life by these two mottos: Deeds, not Words, and For God and my Country. He is affectionately remembered as the father of our nation, commander in chief of the Continental Army during the Revolutionary War, and the first President of the United States.

A telling example of George Washington's character is when he was confronted with the issue of a title. Since there had never been an elected government before, the only thing to which people could relate the office of the supreme commander to was a royal monarchy. At first people thought it was best to call Washington things like *majesty* and *your most highness*. Washington, however, had a different idea. He refused to be called anything except Mr. President. That's the quality of the first leader of the United States. If it had been anyone else, pride (or the desire for power), might have gotten in the way of America's future.

Washington was born in Westmoreland County, Virginia, in the year 1732. He lost his father when he was just a young boy. Soon after, he went to live with his half brother Lawrence at the estate called Mount Vernon. Washington and Lawrence became very close, Lawrence being like a father to George. It was thanks to Lawrence's connections that Washington became a surveyor in the area. Much to his dismay, he lost his brother to tuberculosis in 1752. Following his death, Lawrence's estate, Mount Vernon, passed to George. Washington loved the estate. He would later spend his few years of happy retirement there.

A couple of years later, the French and Indian War broke out in 1754. Thus Washington began his military career, becoming an officer in the British Army. The war came about due to the struggle between France and England over control of colonial lands. Washington's family originally traveled from England to the New World; therefore, his loyalties were to the British Army. Ironically, his experiences as a soldier helped him understand the importance of leadership, and prepared him for his future role fighting against the British.

After a fight called the Battle of the Wilderness, Washington found himself simply grateful to be alive. When the battle started, there were about 1,450 soldiers fighting alongside him. By the end of it, there were about a thousand less. At that time, all officers in the British Army fought on horseback. This made them easy targets for the enemy to shoot down. Though they tried numerous times, Washington could not even find a mark on his skin after the battle. What he did find, however, were bullet holes in his coat. He was the only officer left unharmed. Following the battle Washington wrote a letter to his brother saying this:

> *"By the all-powerful dispensations of Providence I have been protected beyond all human probability or expectation; for I had four bullets through my coat, and two horses shot under me yet escaped unhurt."*

Washington narrowly eluded death many times in his life. Miraculously, he was never injured in all the battles he participated in not only as a soldier, but also as commander of the Continental Army.

Following the French and Indian War, Washington moved home to Mount Vernon, where he took great care in managing the estate. He was elected to the House of Burgesses in 1758, and in 1759, he married Martha Dandridge Curtis, who was the young widow of a well-established member of the community. From the many letters he wrote to Martha we can assume that he cared for her very deeply.

In 1775, war was upon the United States. Congress chose George Washington to defend America and take command of the Continental Army. Some would say that the most powerful contribution Washington ever gave his country was serving as commander in chief during the Revolutionary War. When most people were ready to give up on the revolution, Washington never would. There's no denying that for a time, American Independence seemed like a distant dream that could never be reached. The British Army was known as a worldwide power. What could America do to overcome it? Washington, although I'm sure he had his moments, never let down his men. They believed in themselves because he believed in them. His unconventional strategies saved them more than once, and his unwillingness to give in eventually won the war.

Knowing that the army they were about to face far outnumbered them, George Washington said this to his men before a battle:

> *"Remember, officers and soldiers, that you are freemen fighting for the blessings of liberty."*

Washington knew that this was what set the ragtag American Army apart from the British. If they had any hope of winning the war it was only because they fought for their homes, their loved ones, and their freedom.

There were many defining moments in the American Revolution. One in particular, some refer to as a miracle, or possibly the most daring act in the history of the war. The British were closing in on the Continental Army. Following the Battle of Long Island, America's troops were battered and weak. The British had them surrounded with the East River at their backs. It looked as if the Revolutionary War was about to be over. They were too weak to defeat any attacks. Their only option was retreat. But how? Surely the British would see, or hear, nine thousand men crossing the river. Despite the risks, it was their only chance. Washington gave the order, and the troops prepared for the crossing. At first they had the cover of darkness to conceal them, but the retreat took longer than anticipated. Dawn was nearing, and they knew time was running out. Just as the light was about to expose them, an unusually dense fog began to roll in. Hope swelled within the men. They just might make it. Washington crossed on the very last boat, and with him came a story that would defy explanation. Every single American soldier made it safely across. The British never heard or saw them, and when they went to check on the position of the American soldiers, all they found was an empty camp. Their chance to win the war had slipped away during the night.

Washington eventually learned how to defeat the arrogant British Army. Much to the world's surprise, England surrendered to the far less qualified Continental Army. The Treaty of Paris was signed in 1783, ending the war. Washington had completed his duty.

Following the war he took great delight in coming home to his wife and his farm. He planned to spend the rest of his days enjoying it. His country had a different idea though. Despite his plans to retire, he would end up becoming the first President of the United States, and the only one to ever be unanimously elected.

George Washington set into motion some key practices that still continue today. Seeing the wisdom in having advice from those he trusted, he signed into law the formation of a cabinet so that he would be accountable to others. He could have decided that no one should presume to know better than the President. Instead, he knew that the responsibility on his shoulders was too great to handle alone, and the people of the nation needed a leader who was not afraid to ask for advice.

Some people expected Washington to remain President for the rest of his life, like a king. But Washington knew that anyone in such a guaranteed position would not worry about what the people wanted. You can imagine their surprise when he decided it would be best to serve only two terms, or eight years. Every president after him, except for one, followed the lead of the great George Washington. Congress, seeing the insight in his actions, eventually passed it into law that every President would be limited to only two terms in office.

The quote below is taken from Washington's famous farewell address:

> *"In looking forward to the moment which is intended to terminate the career of my public life, my feelings do not permit me to suspend the deep acknowledgment of that debt of gratitude which I owe to my beloved country for the many honors it has conferred upon me."*

That was the kind of man he was, giving thanks to the country that owed him its freedom. He selflessly served to the best of his ability. He led an army, and he led a country that changed the course of history. He shaped our nation with his character. Had there never been a George Washington, our country could be a very different place.

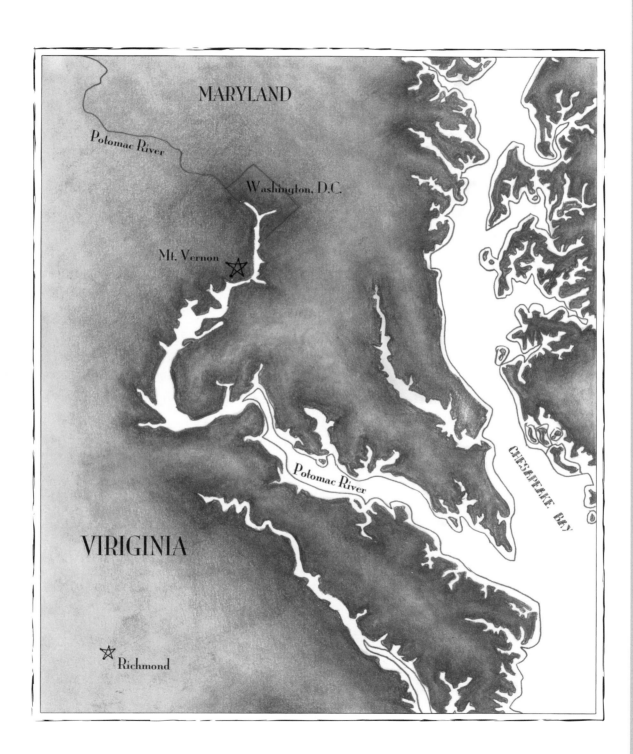

## Discussion

The most remarkable thing about George Washington was that he set a standard for every President with no example to look to for the role of President himself. Can you imagine the amount of responsibility placed on his shoulders? Could you picture yourself having that kind of responsibility? What does it tell you about George Washington that he only wanted to be called "Mr. President" instead of a more grand name?

## Timeline Activity

Put things in perspective. Place George Washington's figure on the timeline in the year 1789, which was when he became our first president. Then identify two other events that happened in history during his life and add them to your timeline. You might also add a symbol or picture that represents this event.

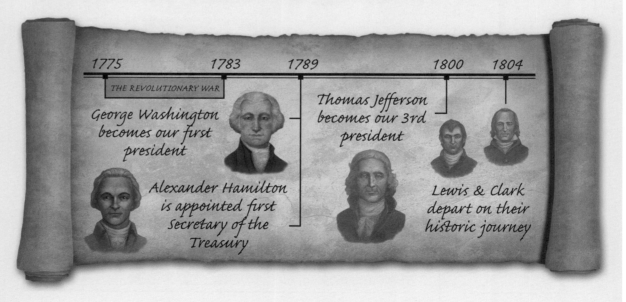

1775          1783          1789               1800     1804

THE REVOLUTIONARY WAR

George Washington becomes our first president

Alexander Hamilton is appointed first Secretary of the Treasury

Thomas Jefferson becomes our 3rd president

Lewis & Clark depart on their historic journey

## *Activity*

One of George Washington's most famous speeches was his farewell address given at the end of his two terms in office. Read the full farewell address given by George Washington. After you've read it a couple times to yourself, read it aloud to your family. Act as though you're Washington giving his final speech.

## *Write a Letter*

If you could speak to George Washington, what would you say? Would you tell him how grateful you are for his sacrifices? Or maybe you would ask him questions about what it was like to do what he did. Write a letter or an email to George Washington. You can also make a postcard instead of writing a letter or email. On your postcard, create a scene that represents the person you read about. Include at least one quote that you think represents this person well.

## *Wordscramble*

Here is a list of scrambled words that relate to the profile you read about George Washington. Unscramble the letters and write the words correctly.

1. enrutoMnoVn _____

2. cfneomnmdarhciie _____

3. otynArCninlatme _____

4. aRntreWvoaioryul _____

5. gtaaygarrm _____

6. taighntnrMosaWah _____

7. itndeeprs _____

8. bCnaeit _____

9. tWnongrGoheegsia _____

10. leasrelaedsfwdr _____

# George Washington Word Search

```
G  F  A  R  E  W  E  L  L  A  D  D  R  E  S  S  U  M  U
Y  Q  F  E  I  H  C  N  I  R  E  D  N  A  M  M  O  C  K
R  A  W  Y  R  A  N  O  I  T  U  L  O  V  E  R  V  J  F
M  A  R  T  H  A  W  A  S  H  I  N  G  T  O  N  D  I  Y
G  E  O  R  G  E  W  A  S  H  I  N  G  T  O  N  Z  N  V
T  T  M  P  I  B  L  V  K  L  U  M  B  M  H  H  O  A  T
G  L  N  M  R  A  G  T  A  G  A  R  M  Y  J  N  P  J  I
G  D  Z  G  U  E  R  C  C  L  X  A  I  Y  R  A  E  F  O
S  N  E  V  N  G  S  L  G  Z  E  Z  K  E  O  F  Q  Q  A
Z  Y  E  J  T  E  N  I  B  A  C  A  V  X  Z  L  O  W  Q
K  K  K  T  U  A  Z  J  D  S  T  T  A  Y  F  X  D  O  H
A  G  H  C  O  N  T  I  N  E  N  T  A  L  A  R  M  Y  I
K  J  S  H  F  T  K  F  J  U  N  R  C  B  G  A  D  F  G
B  Z  Q  L  X  E  A  T  O  N  P  T  H  G  W  J  O  F  H
D  V  M  G  T  L  G  M  O  G  X  Z  E  X  P  F  J  X  U
```

## Word Bank

Cabinet

commander in chief

Continental Army

farewell address

George Washington

Martha Washington

Mount Vernon

president

ragtag army

Revolutionary War

# George Washington Crossword

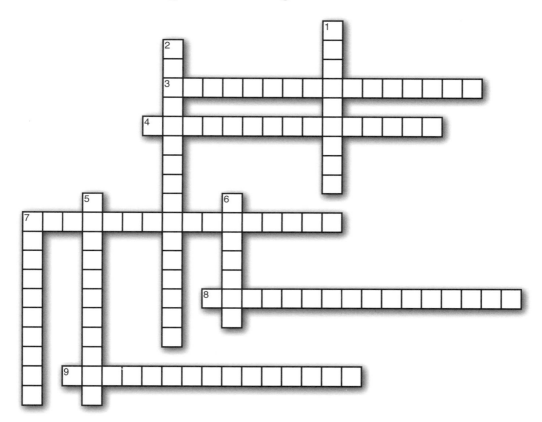

## Across

3. George Washington's wife
4. Washington's final Presidential speech
7. war that led to American independence
8. the first President of the United States
9. American Army

## Down

1. head of the United States
2. leader of the American Army
5. Washington's famous Virginia home
6. committee of advisors to the President
7. nickname for the Continental Army

# Alexander Hamilton

There's something so appealing about the story of an unsung hero. A person who, throughout history, was never remembered quite as he should have been. Life comes with its own set of challenges for each of us. Some choose to never let it defeat them. Alexander Hamilton was one of those. You might recall his name, but do you truly know what he did for this country? Alexander Hamilton is esteemed for being one of our Founding Fathers, and possibly one of the most influential people in the forming of our government. If you happen to have a ten dollar bill nearby, you'll see that Hamilton is one of only two people to ever appear on our common currency without having been President.

Born to an impoverished family in the Caribbean, Alexander Hamilton was forced to become the man of the house at a young age. His father left the family in search of a job and never returned. Alexander's mother was a strong woman who tried her best to repair the broken pieces of her family. Though you might hope no further tragedy would befall the fragile young Hamilton, within two years of his father's desertion, his mother passed away from an unknown illness. Hamilton and his brother were left orphaned and penniless.

With this knowledge of his devastating past, our admiration for Hamilton grows deeper. At the young age of about twelve, he began working for the counting house of Nicholas Cruger and David Beekman. Hamilton quickly showed that he had great promise and a swift wit. This job taught him much about the economic world around him. Working with foreign traders, and at times managing the business, Alexander's experience at the trading company gave him a vast knowledge that would one day prove vital.

As a teenager, Hamilton gained recognition after he wrote a letter that was published in the local newspaper. The letter concerned a terrible hurricane that hit the small island. It was through this exposure that the influential people of St. Croix decided such a promising youth should have the chance to attend college in America. So it was that a gruesome hurricane opened the door to Hamilton's future.

Hamilton attended King's College in New York, which is now known as Columbia University. He had a kind of calm dignity about him. It was his charisma, confidence, and intelligence that often caught the eye of those in authority. He always knew he wanted to do more with his life than what was common. He had a craving for greatness and a yearning to make a difference. So when the Revolutionary War broke out, Hamilton, being fully behind the cause, saw an opportunity.

Through the connections Hamilton had made in New York, he acquired a captaining commission. While Hamilton was still a young leader, Nathaniel Greene, who was one of Washington's most trusted generals, watched with interest as he instructed his troops in their drills. Impressed by their discipline and order, Greene invited the young captain to dinner. Most likely, this is how George Washington first heard the name Alexander Hamilton.

In one letter, Washington wrote, "It is absolutely necessary...for me to have persons that can think for me, as well as execute orders." Hamilton was just the man he needed. After Washington finally took notice of this capable young man, he sent a note inviting him to join his personal staff. In the year 1777, Hamilton began building the most important friendship of his life. At the age of twenty-two he soon became Washington's most trusted aide. One of Washington's gifts was to see the potential in others. He saw a great potential in Alexander. He often referred to him as "my boy." The most cherished leader in America's history began to vastly respect Hamilton's opinion, and even covet his advice. Washington's grand ideas needed Hamilton's capacity to transform them into reality, and Hamilton needed Washington's calm strength to keep him grounded. They made a truly unbeatable team that stood united for over twenty years. With his immense appetite for learning, Hamilton reveled in the opportunity to be mentored by the commander in chief of the Continental Army.

President Washington chose Hamilton to be the very first Secretary of the Treasury. To properly respect this position, you must understand the enormous task Alexander

Hamilton was faced with. He was left with the responsibility of deciding what to do with over 50 million dollars of debt that had accumulated over the course of the war. He was faced with the difficulty of keeping Americans satisfied with their recently acquired liberty from England's over-taxation, and yet still creating a plan that would prosper the nation and pay off its debt. His talent was to see the big picture of America's financial future. He knew that the country needed to build credit and a reliable reputation in the world economy. His plan was to do that at home and abroad by paying back the many people who had supported the country during the war. He needed to create a system that the country could depend on for years to come, which is exactly what he did.

Among Hamilton's other major contributions to America was a set of essays known as *The Federalist Papers*. In Hamilton's home state of New York, people were very critical of the proposed Constitution of the United States. They felt that it infringed on their newfound freedom. So Hamilton decided to write a series of essays that were printed in local newspapers to enlighten the public on the true meaning of the Constitution. Hamilton was not the sole author, but he is credited with writing fifty-one of the eighty-five essays. James Madison, referred to as the Father of the Constitution, contributed about a third, and John Jay, the rest. *The Federalist Papers* are one of Congress's best insights into interpreting the Constitution.

Nothing was ever handed to Alexander Hamilton. He worked hard to be free from the island of his childhood and he strove to impress his teachers at King's College. He knew his future depended on standing out. It was his passion and determination that forced him to push forward in life. Possibly no other acclaimed leader respected Hamilton more than George Washington. If nothing else, that alone is worth admiration. Something most people don't realize is that Alexander actually wrote most of George Washington's famous farewell address.

Despite growing up on an island in the Caribbean with nothing, not even a family to support him, this unsung hero rose above himself for the United States. He saw a cause worth fighting for, and gave everything to pursue it. Though he did not always follow the heroic path in life, he was still a shining beacon of our liberty.

> *"There is a certain enthusiasm in liberty, that makes human nature rise above itself, in acts of bravery and heroism."*
>
> - Alexander Hamilton

# Timeline Activity

Put things in perspective. Place Alexander Hamilton's figure on the timeline in the year 1789, which was when he was appointed America's first Secretary of the Treasury. Then identify two other events that happened in history during his life and add them to your timeline. You might also add a symbol or picture that represents this event.

# Activity

As the first Secretary of the Treasury, Alexander Hamilton nearly single-handedly saved the economy of the United States. Hamilton had to keep in mind taxes, income, expenses, and the other needs of our country. Ask your parent to show you how they keep track of your family's finances. Talk with your parents about your family's income, expenses, and how they keep it all in balance.

## True or False

Create five true or false statements about this story. Present them to your family members. Mix up the true and false statements to keep everyone thinking. Be sure sure to make up an answer key so that your readers will know when they are correct. To see a sample True or False, turn to page 203.

## Wordscramble

Here is a list of scrambled words that relate to the profile you read about Alexander Hamilton. Unscramble the letters and write the words correctly.

1. oWarolnuatRrviye _____

2. rysTuaer _____

3. elCglnoigesK _____

4. orSixtC _____

5. YkwoNer _____

6. riGgennaWhgesoot _____

7. liseedrPrastaFpe _____

8. coomsicen _____

9. iscraamh _____

10. imelnorexAaHnadtl _____

# Using Context

Read the sentence and then look at the word in *italics*. Tell what you think that word means. Then look it up in a dictionary to confirm, or make sure of, the meaning. Tell someone about each word that you got correct. Remember, you will get better at understanding word meanings as you practice using context, or the words around a word.

1. Alexander Hamilton is *esteemed* for being one of our Founding Fathers, and possibly one of the most influential people in the forming of our government. (paragraph 1)

   I think *esteemed* means: _____

   Dictionary definition: _____

   My meaning was: (Circle one)        correct        had correct parts        not close

2. It was his *charisma*, confidence, and intelligence that often caught the eye of those in authority. (paragraph 5)

   I think *charisma* means: _____

   Dictionary definition: _____

   My meaning was: (Circle one)        correct        had correct parts        not close

3. Washington's grand ideas needed Hamilton's *capacity* to transform them into reality, and Hamilton needed Washington's calm strength to keep him grounded. (paragraph 7)

   I think *capacity* means: _____

   Dictionary definition: _____

   My meaning was: (Circle one)        correct        had correct parts        not close

# Alexander Hamilton Word Search

```
F E D E R A L I S T P A P E R S V L F
A W C C T A Q S Y T E Z S E I O E Q W
D M H O K R A A A Z C N A U E O Y W T
G F A O N M E H U E L R L D X U E J G
D U R V E O M A Y Q J R O T N C K Z V
Z B I A Y N M G S J F X D I R G O A V
Z U S U G P E I K U H T X O X V M M F
K E M H V J U W C T R P X B J K A V S
L Y A T Q Y M N Y S Y Y R F R P N O B
V Q R A W Y R A N O I T U L O V E R M
M S N B U Y P O A G R E R D X A R T C
E G E L L O C S G N I K L C R S U L R
N O T L I M A H R E D N A X E L A N K
H G I Y E S B U R L L K M S E Z E N H
A Y G E O R G E W A S H I N G T O N R
```

## Word Bank

Alexander Hamilton

charisma

economics

Federalist Papers

George Washington

King's College

New York

Revolutionary War

St. Croix

Treasury

# Alexander Hamilton Crossword

## Across

3. a set of papers written in defense of the Constitution
4. state with the capitol of Albany
6. the college now known as Columbia University
7. island in the Caribbean Sea where Alexander Hamilton was born
9. first Secretary of the Treasury
10. a quality that attracts and compels confidence

## Down

1. war for American independence
2. Commander of the Continental Army
5. the production, distribution and consumption of goods and services
8. financial department of the United States

# Thomas Hopkins Gallaudet

*"All the children of silence must be taught to sing their own song."*

- Thomas Hopkins Gallaudet

Imagine for a moment that you have suddenly lost the ability to communicate with everyone around you. You can't speak, you can't hear, and you find yourself trapped in silence.

How would you react? It sounds lonely and confusing doesn't it? Think of how many words you use each day to describe what you're feeling, what you want, or need.

Now take a step back in time and imagine that you've been transported to the early 1800s. People assume that since you can't hear or speak, you're not capable of learning or understanding. They think you're ignorant, and you can't tell them otherwise. With nothing else to change your mind, you might even start to believe it too.

Thomas Hopkins Gallaudet understood what it meant to be limited and different from a young age. Thomas grew up always feeling left out. He was plagued with health issues his whole life. He couldn't run with abandon or exert himself without concern. He knew by experience that people usually didn't try to understand another person's differences. They just made their assumptions, or judgments. Maybe that's why, when he saw a young girl playing by herself, he wanted to understand her. She was watching a group of children playing nearby, but not participating.

Alice Cogswell could neither hear nor speak. The reason she wasn't playing with the other children was because she didn't know how. She just watched, maybe daydreaming about the game they were playing, or what it would be like to be one of the normal children.

Thomas walked slowly over to nine-year old Alice. He wasn't apprehensive or hesitant about approaching her like most people she met. Thomas had always reserved a special place in his heart for children, especially children who were misunderstood as he had been. He did what he could to communicate with Alice. Just as he suspected, she was not ignorant like others before him had assumed. Alice was thrilled just to be interacting with someone, anyone. Thomas didn't know exactly how to teach a person he couldn't speak to, but he knew that she had the ability to learn. It was up to him, he decided, to find a way to teach her. Alice Cogswell didn't realize it at the time, but when she met this new friend, her life and the lives of countless others would never be the same.

Thomas Gallaudet was born in Philadelphia, though he spent most of his life in Hartford, Connecticut. Always fighting with his health, Thomas was restricted in what he could do. He was a great student, graduating from Yale at the top of his class. After graduation he began looking for his purpose, trying several things such as law and theology. He even became a traveling salesman. Then he met Alice and everything changed.

Alice's father, who was a prominent doctor in the area, was extremely grateful to Thomas. He had opened the door of communication with his daughter. Together they formed a plan to establish a school for children like Alice. It's hard to believe, but at that time there were no schools for the Deaf in America. Those children were supposedly incapable of learning, remember? In preparation for this new venture Thomas took a trip to Europe at his own expense. He wanted to learn as much as possible from the few schools that taught Deaf children. In France he connected with one teacher in particular, named Laurent Clerc. Laurent was Deaf himself, and trained Thomas in how to communicate with and teach the Deaf.

In April of 1817, the very first school for the Deaf in the United States was opened. Thomas was the principal as well as a teacher. Laurent Clerc, who agreed to return from Europe with Thomas, became the main teacher at the school. It was Alice's father, along with some of his influential friends, who helped make the school a reality with their financial support. In 1817, eight students joined the school. For the first time, they were not just observers of life anymore. They were now able to participate in it.

Being the first school of its kind, people of all ages who wanted to learn were welcome. One such student was nineteen years old when the school first opened. Sophia Fowler loved to learn and couldn't wait to be a part of Thomas's school. Watching others, she had already taught herself how to sew and cook. Thomas couldn't help but fall in love with her spirited personality. The two kept in touch through letters when school was out. Upon Sophia's graduation in 1821, Thomas asked for her hand in marriage. Together, the two would have eight children and enjoy a lovely life. Thomas remained principal of his school until the year 1830. He retired only when his health kept him from continuing. At the time of his departure, the school had grown from eight students to 140.

Taking up his father's cause, Edward Gallaudet and his mother helped found the first college for the Deaf in America. It was called the Columbia Institution for the Deaf and Dumb, located in Washington, D.C. Abraham Lincoln chartered the institution as the National Deaf-Mute College in 1864. The school later changed its name to Gallaudet University, in honor of Thomas.

It's unimaginable to think of all the people who owe their knowledge and their ability to communicate with others to Thomas Gallaudet. No longer were the deaf in America confined to a life of silence. They had hope and a future. Today, there are schools for the Deaf in all fifty states.

Three years after his death, a granite monument was built in Gallaudet's hometown of Hartford, CT, stating this:

ERECTED TO THE MEMORY OF
REV. THOMAS HOPKINS GALLAUDET, LL.D.
BY THE DEAF AND DUMB
OF THE UNITED STATES,
AS A TESTIMONIAL
OF PROFOUND GRATITUDE
TO THEIR
EARLIEST AND BEST FRIEND
AND BENEFACTOR.

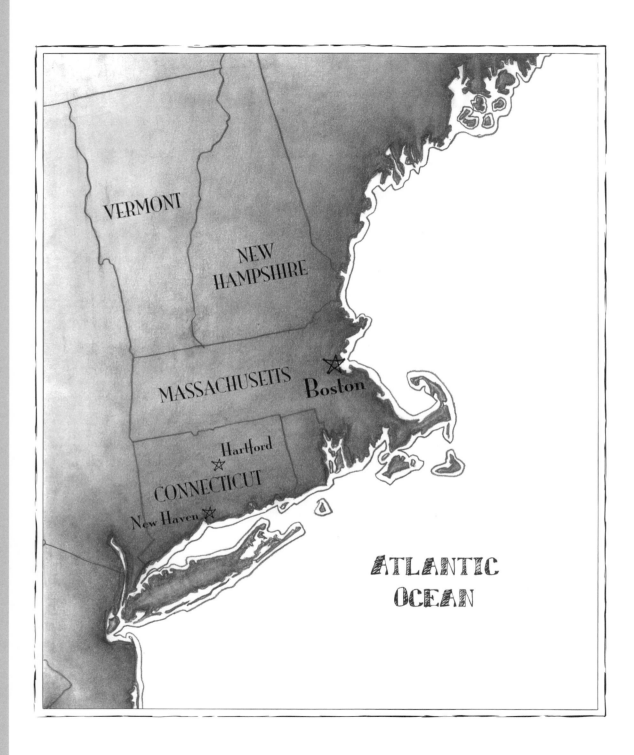

## Discussion

Alice Cogswell attended the very first school for the Deaf in America opened by Thomas Hopkins Gallaudet. What do you think it was like for Alice Cogswell to go from being so different from everyone to being part of a school of children just like her? How do you think this changed Alice's life?

## Timeline Activity

Put things in perspective. Place Thomas Hopkins Gallaudet's figure on the timeline in the year 1817, which was when he helped open the first school for the Deaf in America. Then identify two other events that happened in history during his life and add them to your timeline. You might also add a symbol or picture that represents this event.

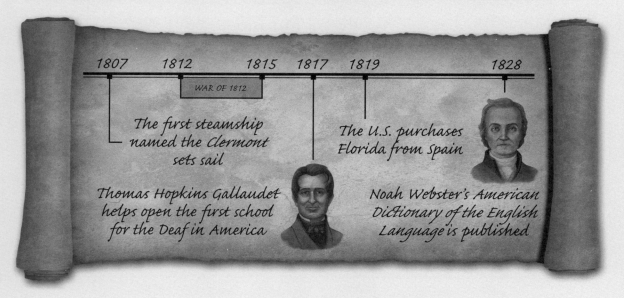

1807    1812        1815    1817    1819              1828

WAR OF 1812

The first steamship named the Clermont sets sail

The U.S. purchases Florida from Spain

Thomas Hopkins Gallaudet helps open the first school for the Deaf in America

Noah Webster's American Dictionary of the English Language is published

## Activity

Thomas Hopkins Gallaudet was a pioneer when it came to educating the Deaf. Sign language was and still is a huge part of Deaf education. Learn the alphabet in sign language, as well as some simple signs for things like "please" and "thank you."

## Wordscramble

Here is a list of scrambled words that relate to the profile you read about Thomas Hopkins Gallaudet. Unscramble the letters and write the words correctly.

1. ialgaugesngn _____
2. uperpos _____
3. lleegCcioslAw _____
4. nsTlstapedakalGhomuiHo _____
5. efda _____

6. CnceLlrrtuea _____
7. hiolaopSFrew _____
8. trarHdfo _____
9. yirrtlnauoeov _____
10. inciparlp _____

## Write an Obituary

Write an obituary or a brief article that would appear about this person upon their passing. Since space is limited in a newspaper you may only use forty to forty-five words to describe this person. With such limited space, focus on the main events in their life. To see a sample obituary, turn to page 203.

# Thomas Hopkins Gallaudet Word Search

```
C V A L I C E C O G S W E L L K L V V
T H T I O B K E I R S H Y S W Q A O G
S J X L T P O P P L Y U I T C J U R W
O K I J K Y L G N X A G L O A O R D K
P D Q C P P U H H N N M Y N H G E Q A
H D V M W R U H Z L Y X P A P A N R F
I I G R D M I R A B W C D G F U T W Z
A X Q G K D Y N P R H O V Y Z C C Z Q
F M F K N S G N C O T X I Y P N L Y V
O Z T I O U P N I S F T R V A E X M
W R M F A S Z I A V P E O N T N R W P
L W X G C K U X K D V A Q R O X C Q Q
E Y E I N W T T Q X Z L L U D Z S C S
R A Y R A N O I T U L O V E R F M I F
U T H O M A S H G A L L A U D E T W K
```

## Word Bank

Alice Cogswell

deaf

Hartford

Laurent Clerc

principal

purpose

revolutionary

sign language

Sophia Fowler

Thomas H. Gallaudet

# Thomas Hopkins Gallaudet Crossword

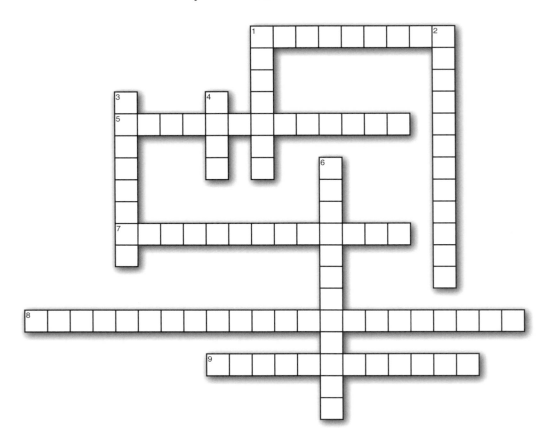

### Across

1. head of a school
5. Thomas Hopkins Gallaudet's first student
7. something that changes the way things are done
8. man who opened the first Deaf school in America
9. Deaf student who became Thomas Hopkins Gallaudet's wife

### Down

1. a reason for doing something or having a sense of mission
2. teacher at the first school for the Deaf from Europe
3. capitol of Connecticut
4. the state of not being able to hear
6. the language used by Deaf people to communicate

# Noah Webster

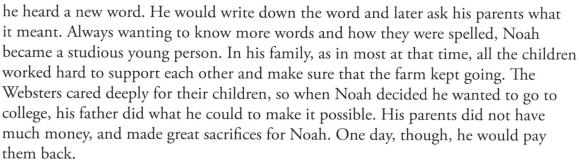

America today has a culture all its own. We have music, fashion, sports, and a lifestyle that is unlike any other place. Noah Webster lived during a time when America was searching for its identity. The revolution won, the colonies were no longer under British rule. It was now time to develop a strictly American way of life. The textbooks used in his day had all been brought over from England. They were not created by Americans or for Americans. Noah Webster decided to take it upon himself to change that.

Born on a farm in West Hartford, Connecticut, young Noah Webster was always fascinated with words. He kept a small notebook with him at all times in case he heard a new word. He would write down the word and later ask his parents what it meant. Always wanting to know more words and how they were spelled, Noah became a studious young person. In his family, as in most at that time, all the children worked hard to support each other and make sure that the farm kept going. The Websters cared deeply for their children, so when Noah decided he wanted to go to college, his father did what he could to make it possible. His parents did not have much money, and made great sacrifices for Noah. One day, though, he would pay them back.

After some tutoring from the local reverend, Noah was accepted to Yale University at the age of sixteen. It was a proud day for the Websters when Noah left for college. He attended Yale during the tumultuous years of the Revolutionary War. Believing strongly in the cause of American freedom, he served as a soldier in his father's company when time allowed.

Following his college years, Noah became a teacher. As a student and a teacher, he realized more and more that America's system of education needed improvement. Not only was it still using textbooks from England, but Noah believed there was a better way to teach. He stated, *"To educate children well is one of the most important duties of parents and guardians."* When he was in school as a boy, he would often get punished for not doing something exactly as he was told. Noah thought this was too harsh and uninspiring. Instead of punishing his students, Noah rewarded them for good behavior. He found this to be a much more effective approach.

In 1789, Noah found love. He married Rebecca Greenleaf, and together they had eight children. Though Noah seemed to be always working on a project, speaking, or writing towards a goal, he loved family life. He used to keep raisins and peppermints in his pockets for his children.

Noah Webster decided to create a tool for learning that could be used all over the country. It taught grammar, spelling, and reading in a uniform way. Up until books like this, teachers used whatever they had or could find. It was in 1783 that Noah wrote a textbook called *A Grammatical Institute of the English Language*. It would become the most popular American book of its time. Teachers all over the states used it in their classrooms. Even Benjamin Franklin taught his granddaughter how to read using it. Many called it the "Blue-Backed Speller" because it had a blue cover. Children in America learned how to read, spell, and pronounce their words for about a hundred years with Noah's help.

The greatest contribution Noah Webster gave to our country took him twenty-seven years to complete. Believing that America needed a universal book of reference for the English Language, Noah spent those years researching and compiling America's first dictionary. He travelled all over, studying the Americanized English language. He asked farmers and statesmen alike for their opinions, trying his best to be true to the people. He even travelled to Europe, spending countless hours examining the original meaning of words. He went to libraries in France and England, learning twenty-six different languages to better understand the words he studied. Noah Webster did all of this work by himself. He stayed focused on the goal and that kept him going. Finally, at the age of seventy, Noah finished his greatest work. The *American Dictionary of the English Language* included seventy thousand words. If you look in your home, you will most likely find a dictionary with his name on it. Now, every time you look up a word, remember the sacrifice and the time that went into the first American dictionary.

It is thanks to Noah that we spell words like *color* with just an o instead of *colour* which is the British version. Another example is the word *public* instead of the British *publick*, or *center* instead of *centre*. Noah also added some words that were not yet in any dictionary, such as *skunk*, *squash*, and *hickory*.

Below is an excerpt from the preface of Noah Webster's dictionary:

> *"It is not only important, but in a degree necessary, that the people of this country should have an American Dictionary of the English Language; for, although the body of the language is the same as in England, and it is desirable to perpetrate that sameness, yet some differences must exist. Language is the expression of ideas; and if the people of one country can not preserve an identity of ideas, they can not retain an identity of language."*

Noah Webster greatly impacted the knowledge of this country. He has been called the "Father of American Scholarship and Education." He created a culture for speaking, spelling, and learning that was American in nature. Classrooms were now free of the outdated British textbooks they had been using. Webster referred to his achievements as *"American books, for American children."* Among other things, Noah studied law and was admitted to the bar in 1781, helped found Amherst College in Massachusetts, began the first daily newspaper in New York, fought for copyright laws, helped found the Connecticut Society for the Abolition of Slavery, and is most remembered as America's leading lexicographer. Not quite sure what that word means? Maybe you should look it up!

## Discussion

Noah Webster lived at a time when America was creating its own culture. If you could speak with him today, what would you tell Noah has changed in America's culture now versus when he was alive? Do you think he would approve of all the changes? Why, or why not?

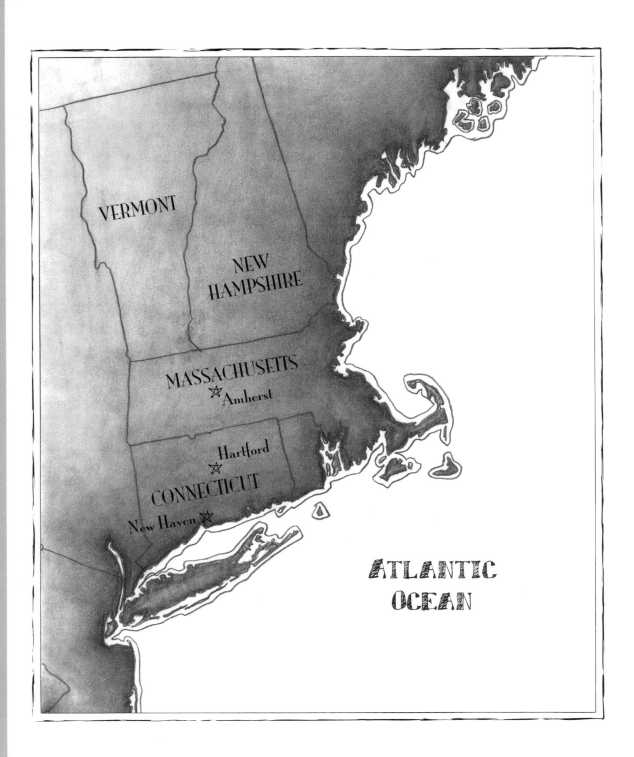

## Timeline Activity

Put things in perspective. Place Noah Webster's figure on the timeline in the year 1828, when his book *American Dictionary of the English Language* was published. Then identify two other events that happened in history during his life and add them to your timeline. You might also add a symbol or picture that represents this event.

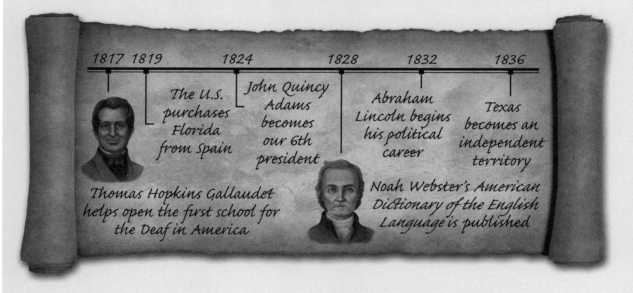

1817   1819          1824               1828          1832          1836

The U.S. purchases Florida from Spain

John Quincy Adams becomes our 6th president

Abraham Lincoln begins his political career

Texas becomes an independent territory

Thomas Hopkins Gallaudet helps open the first school for the Deaf in America

Noah Webster's American Dictionary of the English Language is published

## Activity

In honor of Noah Webster, keep your own personal dictionary for a week. Carry around a small notebook, just like Noah, and every time you hear or read a new word, write it in your notebook. Next time you have the chance, look up the meaning of that word and write it in your notebook. See how many new words you can learn in one week.

## Wordscramble

Here is a list of scrambled words that relate to the profile you read about Noah Webster. Unscramble the letters and write the words correctly.

1. aelY _____

2. ahrtcee _____

3. rsNtehoWabe _____

4. paroelchxeirg _____

5. ortindciay _____

6. trdHfrao _____

7. lespler _____

8. GaceRefblncaeree _____

9. oxotetbk _____

10. esnpraeervce _____

## Using Context

Read the sentence and then look at the word in *italics*. Tell what you think that word means. Then look it up in a dictionary to confirm, or make sure of, the meaning. Tell someone about each word that you got correct. Remember, you will get better at understanding word meanings as you practice using context, or the words around a word.

1. America today has a *culture* all its own. (paragraph 1)

   I think *culture* means: _____

   Dictionary definition: _____

   My meaning was: (Circle one)        correct        had correct parts        not close

2. Always wanting to know more words and how they were spelled, Noah became a *studious* young person. (paragraph 2)

   I think *studious* means: _____

   Dictionary definition: _____

   My meaning was: (Circle one)        correct        had correct parts        not close

3. The greatest *contribution* Noah Webster gave to our country took him twenty-seven years to complete. (paragraph 7)

   I think *contribution* means: _____

   Dictionary definition: _____

   My meaning was: (Circle one)        correct        had correct parts        not close

# Noah Webster Word Search

```
C D O Z A K V S Q N B C P T L K D B G
Q O G J G H N R W J A I R Q O A I H H
R P W U A P E R A M T D Y M M X W F P
W D O K W H A R T F O R D Y T J J X E
G E C A C G Q D I C T I O N A R Y M R
K F F A E L N E E R G A C C E B E R S
S P E L L E R P F C H Z J P O G T O E
K T H R P Y J T O Z M Z E Q W E W Y V
P W O H J D X T K O M R D D X M T T E
Z J Y A I N R X K D R D Y T B Q G L R
Z U F E Z G M X F R B W B R L U B W A
V Q K L R E H P A R G O C I X E L I N
M R G A A T J X S M O E E C H E Y V C
R Y P Y K J W R E K W V A M G U R Y E
R E T S B E W H A O N A R T H K R Q N
```

## Word Bank

dictionary

Hartford

lexicographer

Noah Webster

perseverance

Rebecca Greenleaf

speller

teacher

textbook

Yale

# *Noah Webster Crossword*

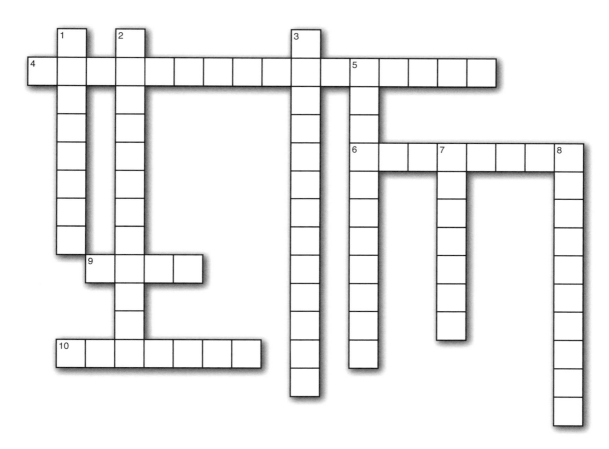

## Across

4. the wife of Noah Webster
6. the capitol of Connecticut
9. Ivy League college in Connecticut
10. a book that teaches spelling

## Down

1. a book used to teach a specific subject
2. the persistence of doing a thing despite difficulty
3. someone who compiles dictionaries
5. man who compiled the first American dictionary
7. instructor in education
8. a book that lists words and their meanings

# William McGuffey

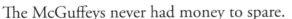

William McGuffey grew up in a backwoods region near Youngstown, Ohio. The McGuffeys were moral people who went to church and worked hard on their farm. William's father was an excellent outdoorsman, and was known throughout the county for his shooting skills, but William didn't take after his father. He loved to read with his mother, and learn his letters. As soon as his chores were finished William wanted more than anything to learn and read. William's mother was proud of his quick mind, and enjoyed working with him. He could easily memorize huge portions of books. William's mother wanted him to one day use his talents to become a minister.

The McGuffeys never had money to spare. With school being so expensive for a small family of farmers, it took many years before William was able to work his way to a college degree. Finally though, William graduated from the nearby Washington College with honors in 1826. It had been a long journey. After learning all he could from his mother, William was tutored by the local minister for a couple of years, working at his house to pay for lodging. Next, he went to Old Stone Academy where he spent several years preparing for college. Throughout that time, William had to interrupt his education by taking jobs as a teacher to pay for his schooling.

It was while William was teaching at a private school in Kentucky that the president of Miami University (in Ohio) first spotted him. The president, impressed by his teaching, recommended William for a professorship at the university. So the following year, William, along with his then ten-year old brother Aleck, headed off to Oxford,

Ohio. He had offered to take his brother with him in order to tutor Aleck and lessen his mother's burdens at home. William served as Miami University's professor of languages.

While at the university, William met a young woman by the name of Harriet Spining. She was the daughter of a well-respected judge from the Dayton area of Ohio. The two fell in love and were married in the spring of 1827. William and Harriet had five children together.

William McGuffey started holding reading classes in front of his home in Ohio. He loved taking strides toward understanding how young students learned best. These days of observing children surely contributed to the *McGuffey Readers* he would later be known for. William spent ten years at Miami University. During that time he became a member of the College of Professional Teachers of the Western Country, and in 1829 was ordained as a minister. It was just as his mother had always hoped. William was a prolific and enthusiastic preacher.

In 1836, William McGuffey resigned his professorship at Miami University, moving on to become president of Cincinnati College. Mostly due to the school's financial troubles, William resigned in 1839. He then became the president of Ohio University. This too proved to be only a short employment. Afterwards, while teaching at Woodward College, William accepted a professorship position at the University of Virginia. Founded by Thomas Jefferson, this university was one of the best schools in the country. William taught in Virginia for the next twenty-eight years. Always striving for students who would think for themselves and not just repeat information, William prodded his classes with questions. Many students loved William's classes, some feared them, but all respected the teacher.

William McGuffey is best remembered for his readers. First published in 1836, William's textbooks, or primers, were used in most schools across the country for many, many years. They taught reading, spelling, vocabulary, and lessons of morality. Five generations of Americans were shaped by these lessons. It is estimated that 120 million copies of the *McGuffey Readers* were sold. William's goal was to help young students connect to what they were learning while also instilling values in them. Patriotism, honesty, and discipline were just some of the principles on which he focused. He used stories of animals and children to illustrate his lessons. McGuffey also made sure to use examples that most children could understand such as "A is for Ax" and "B is for Box." He even included rhymes and verses that he thought would be easy to remember. Things like:

*The lark is up to meet the sun,*
*The bee is on the wing,*
*The ant his labor has begun,*
*The woods with music ring.*
*Shall bird, and bee, and ant, be wise,*
*While I my moments waste?*
*Oh, let me with the morning rise*
*And to my duties haste.*

One of McGuffey's many fans, Henry Ford, felt that the readers he had once read as a boy were so important that he republished them at his own expense. He distributed them to schools across the country, hoping that children would be as inspired by them as he was.

William McGuffey devoted his life to education. He had a love for learning, and later a love for teaching. He is remembered as the Great Schoolmaster of the Nation. Upon his death the National Education Association honored William McGuffey, stating:

*"In the death of William H. McGuffey, late professor of moral philosophy in the University of Virginia, this Association feels that they have lost one of the great lights of the profession whose life was a lesson full of instruction; an example and model to American teachers."*

## Discussion

Imagine that everyone in the country is learning to read with the same book. Could this create any problems? What if the book was too hard for someone to use? Could everyone having the same book create any benefits? Would it encourage everyone to have the same beliefs? Reread the rhyme in William McGuffey's profile. What do you think William McGuffey is trying to instill with this rhyme? Do you agree with him? Why, or why not?

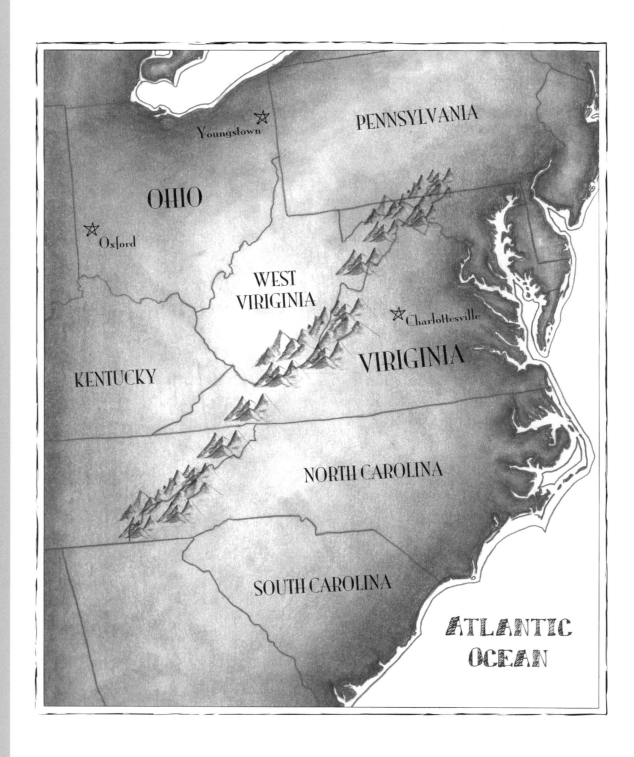

## Timeline Activity

Put things in perspective. Place William McGuffey's figure on the timeline in the year 1836, which was when the first publication of the *McGuffey Readers* came out. Then identify two other events that happened in history during his life and add them to your timeline. You might also add a symbol or picture that represents this event.

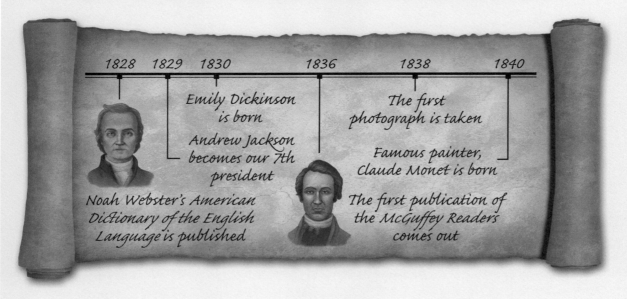

1828   1829   1830        1836        1838        1840

Emily Dickinson is born

Andrew Jackson becomes our 7th president

Noah Webster's American Dictionary of the English Language is published

The first photograph is taken

Famous painter, Claude Monet is born

The first publication of the McGuffey Readers comes out

## Activity

William McGuffey used his readers to teach valuable lessons in a way that children could grasp. Write a short children's story using the characters and scenarios to illustrate a moral lesson, such as "Why not to lie" or "How you can help." You may want to illustrate your story.

# True or False

Create five true or false statements about this story. Present them to your family members. Mix up the true and false statements to keep everyone thinking. Be sure sure to make up an answer key so that your readers will know when they are correct. To see a sample True or False, turn to page 203.

# Write a Letter

If you could speak to William McGuffey, what would you say? Would you tell him how grateful you are for his sacrifices? Or maybe you would ask him questions about what it was like to do what he did. Write a letter or an email to William McGuffey. You can also make a postcard instead of writing a letter or email. On your postcard, create a scene that represents the person you read about. Include at least one quote that you think represents this person well.

# Wordscramble

Here is a list of scrambled words that relate to the profile you read about William McGuffey. Unscramble the letters and write the words correctly.

1. eHritainirSgnp _____
2. oOih _____
3. WcfafGmyeMliilu _____
4. ufrdaGeRyscefMe _____
5. slamor _____

6. srorsfpeo _____
7. stUyvinrie _____
8. kototebx _____
9. rtiensmi _____
10. rehscatooslm _____

# William McGuffey Word Search

```
M  J  Y  E  F  F  U  G  C  M  M  A  I  L  L  I  W  T  O
S  S  P  C  F  R  S  K  W  P  I  O  P  U  U  H  Y  S  P
L  E  P  T  N  I  S  B  X  N  M  N  I  V  A  X  Q  A  M
S  N  V  E  F  Q  F  U  O  I  F  T  I  R  B  M  W  D  W
Y  B  L  X  U  R  V  X  C  T  D  H  R  S  G  G  K  I  X
K  J  X  T  V  G  V  O  I  H  O  I  H  E  T  L  G  R  Z
K  T  H  B  G  T  X  R  Q  L  E  H  Z  K  V  E  V  K  U
S  C  H  O  O  L  M  A  S  T  E  R  M  F  G  T  R  A  M
W  D  O  O  Y  C  T  B  S  M  Y  O  D  R  V  Y  D  O  G
Y  O  I  K  I  G  P  R  O  F  E  S  S  O  R  B  N  U
I  V  T  R  U  N  I  V  E  R  S  I  T  Y  Z  H  Q  Z  B
S  Q  Z  L  G  N  Z  A  S  A  S  Q  P  I  X  K  Y  C  Z
M  P  I  Q  I  R  Q  U  R  L  K  K  L  K  I  F  W  P  R
C  S  A  N  H  R  M  Y  L  S  Q  C  O  V  K  B  N  Q  V
Z  B  G  S  R  E  D  A  E  R  Y  E  F  F  U  G  C  M  Z
```

## Word Bank

| | |
|---|---|
| Harriet Spining | professor |
| McGuffey Readers | schoolmaster |
| minister | textbook |
| morals | University |
| Ohio | William McGuffey |

# William McGuffey Crossword

## Across

4. author of the McGuffey Readers
5. a person's standards in the way they act or behave
6. set of readers written to instruct children to read
7. a book used to teach a specific subject
9. university founded by Thomas Jefferson

## Down

1. another word for preacher
2. wife of William McGuffey
3. term used for school teacher during the 1800s
8. a college teacher
10. state where William McGuffey was born

# Harriet Beecher Stowe

**H**ave you ever been moved to tears, anger, or action by something you read?

Many years ago, there was a time when only a few in our country acknowledged the deep injustice of slavery, and believed it should be outlawed. As such, many pieces had to fall into place for this country to give up the bonds of slavery. One terrible war was the deciding factor. Someone, though, had to be the spark that would ignite a fire.

Harriet Beecher was born in Connecticut in the year 1811. She was the seventh child of a big family. Her father was a preacher. He always encouraged his children in education and in life. Harriet found that from a young age, she loved to read and write. She loved great stories and poetry. In 1834, she won a writing contest for a magazine. Soon after, she started writing articles and stories for other magazines. A couple of years later, Harriet married a man named Calvin Ellis Stowe. Calvin was a professor at her father's theological seminary. He was a great supporter of her writing. Together, they would have seven children of their own.

Does everything happen for a reason? Harriet Beecher Stowe believed so. She believed that she was meant to do something more with her writing. Her heart yearned to expose the truth about slavery. She had seen with her own eyes the unbearable acts that the majority of America refused to stand against. She knew of the destruction that it caused. People were being treated like objects, things without souls that you could buy and sell. From a mother's perspective, Harriet couldn't understand how families were torn apart without a second thought. How could that be America? How could this same country possibly bear the title land of the free? And most of all, what could she do about it?

In 1850, the Fugitive Slave Act was passed and Harriet watched with disbelief as slaves who had escaped their chains were now being hunted down and returned. Soon after that, when she was in church one Sunday, she had a vision. She said it inspired her to write *Uncle Tom's Cabin*.

> *"I could not control the story, the Lord himself wrote it, I was but an instrument in His hands and to Him should be given all the praise."*

Harriet had found her calling. She found her way to make a difference. You see, many believe it was the book she wrote that ignited the fire. In it, you read about several different slaves, their journeys, and the various types of people around them. The good owner has to sell two of his slaves to survive. The cruel one is the worst kind of owner, and there are varying levels of racism found in between. It is a story of love, loss, malice, forgiveness, and faith.

As people read it, their eyes were opened. It gave anyone who had never owned a slave before, or even seen slavery, a clear picture of what it meant. People were moved to tears, to anger, and most importantly, to action.

The main character in *Uncle Tom's Cabin*, Uncle Tom, is brutally and wrongfully killed at the end of the book, murdered by his cruel and unforgiving master.

Harriet didn't write that ending so that people would be overcome with sadness, she wrote it so that they would stand up for what is right. Those who would fight in and eventually win the Civil War needed to have a passion burning inside them. They needed something worth risking their lives for.

Wars have been won and lost over the passion of the soldiers who fought in them. If they did not believe in what they were fighting for, the cause was already lost. Many have wondered how the American Army overcame the much more powerful, and much more experienced, British Army. They won for several reasons, but possibly the most important was that those in the Continental Army fought for their freedom, their homes, and for their families. They were ready and willing to risk life itself for such a worthy cause.

Harriet knew that if everyone could just grasp the immensity of the injustice, if they could just imagine themselves in such circumstances, they might be outraged enough to do something about it.

*Uncle Tom's Cabin* gave everyone who read it a personal experience with slavery. Most people who lived in free states at that time had never seen the horrors of slavery with their own eyes. They might have heard a story here, or seen a refugee there, but they didn't know first hand. Harriet wanted them to feel what the slaves felt, to see what they saw. She wanted them to have a glimpse of the fear, the hatred, and the hopelessness of slavery.

At first, the book was published as a weekly series in the magazine called *The National Era*. After some installments of the series, people started to take notice. A publisher in Boston decided to take a chance on Harriet. Once the book was released in 1852 they could not print it fast enough to meet the demand. *Uncle Tom's Cabin* is considered the best selling novel of the 19th century. The success of the book catapulted Stowe into worldwide fame, and reserved her a place in history.

In 1862, Harriet had the opportunity to meet President Abraham Lincoln. It is said that when he met her he joked, "So you're the little woman who wrote the book that started this great war!"

Harriet Beecher Stowe never fought in the Civil War. She never fired a rifle, or helped win a battle, but she was a true hero of it. She shined a light in the darkness, and rallied a nation to action. Americans were no longer willing to silently accept slavery. They fought with passion and fire, because their eyes had been opened and they knew the truth.

In a poem written about Harriet, the famous John G. Whittier says it best:

> *"She needs no guarantee of fame*
> *Whose own is linked with Freedom's name"*

Harriet wrote many other books in her lifetime, although none ever as popular, or as influential, as *Uncle Tom's Cabin*. She was eighty-five years old when she died at her home in Hartford, Connecticut. Now, her house is called The Harriet Beecher Stowe Center. It is dedicated to promoting her beliefs and remembering a life well spent.

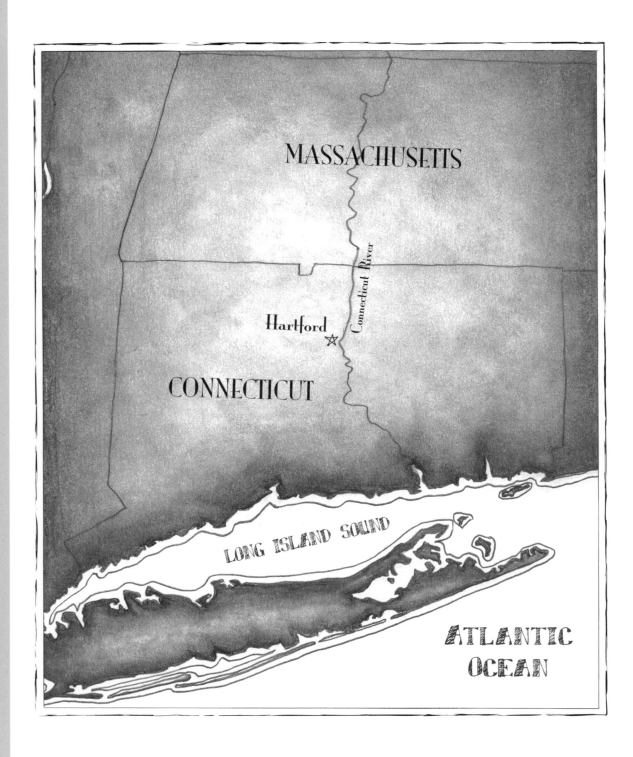

## Discussion

Harriet Beecher Stowe wanted to make a difference with her life. The injustice of slavery burned inside of her and she did what she could to stop it. Is there anything that makes you feel that way? If so, explain why. With your parents' help, think of some ways that you might be able to make a difference.

## Timeline Activity

Put things in perspective. Place Harriet Beecher Stowe's figure on the timeline in the year 1852, which was when *Uncle Tom's Cabin* was published. Then identify two other events that happened in history during his life and add them to your timeline. You might also add a symbol or picture that represents this event.

1844 — First telegraph sent by Samuel Morse

1850 — Harriet Tubman helps her first group of slaves to freedom

1852 — Uncle Tom's Cabin is published

1861 — Abraham Lincoln becomes our 16th president

U.S. CIVIL WAR

1865

1867 — U.S. purchases Alaska

## Activity

Laws were passed that affected slaves even if they were not in the South. Learn more about the Fugitive Slave Act. What did it mean? Who instigated the act and why? Do you agree with the Fugitive Slave Act? What do you think you would have done if you had encountered a slave who had escaped his masters?

## Wordscramble

Here is a list of scrambled words that relate to the profile you read about Harriet Beecher Stowe. Unscramble the letters and write the words correctly.

1. odaHftrr _____

2. AegeiFuivtalSctv _____

3. iUbcenmlaoCnTs _____

4. iisnvo _____

5. arlantaNoEi _____

6. ivlaCirW _____

7. LcmhnAaalinrob _____

8. hcHeteaeiSwBrortree _____

9. tifah _____

10. ruhato _____

# Using Context

Read the sentence and then look at the word in *italics*. Tell what you think that word means. Then look it up in a dictionary to confirm, or make sure of, the meaning. Tell someone about each word that you got correct. Remember, you will get better at understanding word meanings as you practice using context, or the words around a word.

1. Many years ago, there was a time when only a few in our country *acknowledged* the deep injustice of slavery, and believed it should be outlawed. (paragraph 2)

   I think *acknowledged* means: _____

   Dictionary definition: _____

   My meaning was: (Circle one)    correct    had correct parts    not close

2. Her heart *yearned* to expose the truth about slavery. (paragraph 4)

   I think *yearned* means: _____

   Dictionary definition: _____

   My meaning was: (Circle one)    correct    had correct parts    not close

3. Harriet knew that if everyone could just grasp the *immensity* of the injustice, if they could just imagine themselves in such circumstances, they might be outraged enough to do something about it. (paragraph 12)

   I think *immensity* means: _____

   Dictionary definition: _____

   My meaning was: (Circle one)    correct    had correct parts    not close

# Harriet Beecher Stowe Word Search

```
C B N O S N P P D M P V G S T G U E S
U N C L E T O M S C A B I N G B A W S
Q B L I O O G I K F I D R B B Y R O I
T A K C V C J Q P W M R T T V L E T N
F H E X T U N C T W O O U O O R L S E
G Z N Q A D U I W E S F A I T H A B R
T M M U F S R C L X M T X Q T E N T U
S M H M S S P A M M M R I C Y S O E V
U B V G N L Z H W D A A Z R M P I I E
G K K T M O S U F L L H U A Y T T R X
O O A I G W I H P N I K A T X Z A R L
V M T E M P R S G H L V P R H N N A P
Z Y W G L R J W I O T G I I B O B H X
Z H R Q E U V B E V R W Y C J A R X C
N F U G I T I V E S L A V E A C T Z U
```

## Word Bank

Abraham Lincoln
author
Civil War
faith
Fugitive Slave Act

Harriet B. Stowe
Hartford
National Era
*Uncle Tom's Cabin*
vision

# Harriet Beecher Stowe Crossword

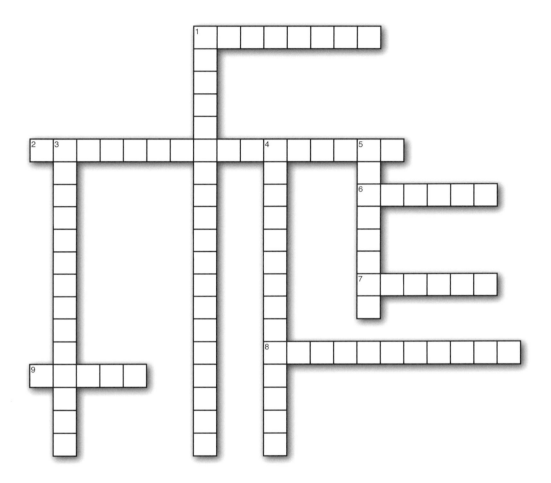

## Across

1. Harriet Beecher Stowe's hometown in CT
2. an act that forced all escaped slaves to return
6. a mental image of a scene
7. writer of a book
8. the magazine that first published *Uncle Tom's Cabin* in installments
9. a strong belief in something

## Down

1. author of *Uncle Tom's Cabin*
3. book that greatly impacted the nation before the Civil War
4. 16th President of the United States
5. the war fought in America between the North and the South

# Abraham Lincoln

Presidents seem to age twice as fast as everyone else. Usually if a president starts his term with few grey hairs, or none at all, he will have gained plenty by the end. Just think of it. The President of the United States has to be continually on call, ready to give a statement or a speech at a moment's notice, and most of all, he has the weight of an entire nation on his shoulders.

There were some presidents, though, who inherited an even more enormous task than most. Perhaps it was President Abraham Lincoln who stepped into the most difficult time our country has ever seen. The sixteenth President of the United States was faced with Civil War—a country fighting against itself.

During his first inaugural address, Lincoln said this of his impending role:

> *"Fifteen different and greatly distinguished citizens have in succession administered the executive branch of Government. They have conducted it through many perils, and generally with great success. Yet, with all this scope of precedent, I now enter upon the same task for the brief constitutional term of four years under great and peculiar difficulty."*

Lincoln knew of the coming destruction to the nation if it did not at last come together and put aside any idea of violence. His entire inaugural address was a plea to preserve the Union. Those in the north end of our country could not have been happier that Lincoln was elected president. People in the south, however, felt that since their choice for president had lost, their voice and their rights were lost with him. In the excerpt below from the same address, Lincoln tried to assure them that this was not so:

> *"We are not enemies, but friends. We must not be enemies. Though passion may have strained it must not break our bonds of affection. The mystic chords of memory, stretching from every battlefield and patriot grave to every living heart and hearthstone all over this broad land, will yet swell the chorus of the Union, when again touched, as surely they will be, by the better angels of our nature."*

Unfortunately, his pleas fell on deaf ears. The Union would stand again, but not without a brutal war being fought first. The war lasted much longer than anyone could have imagined, and killed many more people than anyone could have thought.

The battle of Gettysburg was one of the most important of the Civil War. Taking place a little over two years into the conflict, it not only was a significant turning point toward northern victory, but it was also one of the bloodiest battles of the entire war. More than fifty thousand soldiers were killed, injured or went missing. On November 19, 1863, a ceremony was held to dedicate the cemetery at Gettysburg. A man named Edward Everett, who was a famous orator of his time, was scheduled to be the main speaker at the event. His speech was over two hours long. Once he had finished, Lincoln stood up in front of the 15,000 people who had gathered. His task was to share just a few final remarks. President Lincoln only spoke for two minutes. As it turns out, that was all the time he needed to deliver a speech that is remembered as one of the best ever written. The Gettysburg Address is now inscribed at the Lincoln memorial in Washington D.C. It is widely revered for its simple, but meaningful eloquence. In it, Lincoln did not focus on who was to blame for the lives that had been lost. Instead, he reminded the nation of what could possibly be worth so much devastation. Below is the opening sentence:

> *"Fourscore and seven years ago our fathers brought forth on this continent a new nation, conceived in liberty, and dedicated to the proposition that all men are created equal."*

The South could never have defeated the cause of freedom. Abraham Lincoln is remembered as the Liberator, or the Great Emancipator. He gave an estimated four million slaves a new life. Imagine the excitement, and the disbelief when the

Emancipation Proclamation was first issued by Lincoln. Slaves who could read, read for themselves the incredible news. Those who couldn't gathered together while someone else read it aloud. What a moment it must have been, to realize that you were no longer *owned* by someone else, but free. Understand that it was not easy, or popular, for President Lincoln to make the decisions that he made. In the end, he was murdered because of them. He knew that with such change would come great opposition. He accepted the repercussions because it was bigger than he. Freedom was on the line.

Lincoln realized that bitterness was just as treacherous a foe as violence. He knew that it could destroy the nation just as easily. The statement below is from President Lincoln's Second Inaugural Address. In it, he was pleading with the country again. This time with the Civil War almost at its end, he was begging for the people to let bitterness fade away, and healing begin.

> *"With malice toward none, with charity for all, with firmness in the right as God gives us to see the right, let us strive on to finish the work we are in, to bind up the nation's wounds, to care for him who shall have borne the battle and for his widow and his orphan, to do all which may achieve and cherish a just and lasting peace among ourselves and with all nations."*

I wish Abraham Lincoln had lived long enough to see all that he accomplished. I wish he had survived so that the reconstruction and uniting of our nation would have been in the hands of one of America's greatest presidents. Instead, he was stolen from us, his life and his legacy cut short. I'm not sure that he ever knew how important he was to our country. During his presidency Lincoln had to deal with many criticisms. He even had to accept the fact that half of the country, if not more, vehemently opposed him, seceding from his command and electing their own President. If only he could have known how much his country would one day treasure what he did. If he could see his face carved into the side of a mountain, or know that almost every school in America would have its students memorize his speeches because they were so important, and so powerful. I wish he could see the memorial that was built for him in our nation's capital. It is a symbol of his legacy that will forever stand for freedom and liberty.

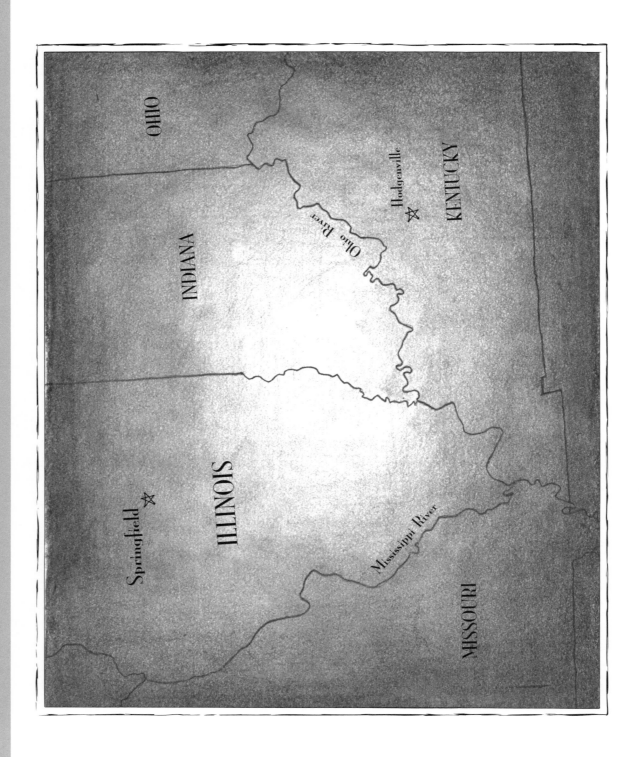

## Discussion

Abraham Lincoln gave some of the most eloquent and powerful speeches in our nation's history. Reread the four quotes given by Abraham Lincoln in his profile. Which one is your favorite? Tell your family which quote is your favorite and why. Read the whole speech that your favorite quote was taken from. You may want to share this speech with your family.

## Timeline Activity

Put things in perspective. Place Abraham Lincoln's figure on the timeline in the year 1861, which was when he became the 16th president of the United States. Then identify two other events that happened in history during his life and add them to your timeline. You might also add a symbol or picture that represents this event.

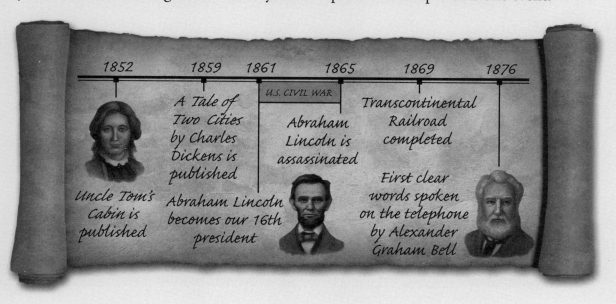

1852 — Uncle Tom's Cabin is published

1859 — A Tale of Two Cities by Charles Dickens is published / Abraham Lincoln becomes our 16th president

1861 — U.S. CIVIL WAR

1865 — Abraham Lincoln is assassinated

1869 — Transcontinental Railroad completed / First clear words spoken on the telephone by Alexander Graham Bell

1876

## Activity

Abraham Lincoln is one of four Presidents that were carved into Mount Rushmore. Learn about this monumental feat. Where is it located? How long did it take to complete? Who built it, and why? Do you find it inspiring to look at? Tell your family what you learn about Mt. Rushmore.

## Write an Obituary

Write an obituary or a brief article that would appear about this person upon their passing. Since space is limited in a newspaper you may only use forty to forty-five words to describe this person. With such limited space, focus on the main events in their life. To see a sample obituary, turn to page 203.

## Wordscramble

Here is a list of scrambled words that relate to the profile you read about Abraham Lincoln. Unscramble the letters and write the words correctly.

1. ilrWCvai _____

2. bysuetsedgrGstrAd _____

3. irpetsdne _____

4. oEmlotaimoaiaatcrpiPnnnc _____

5. LlcobianmaArnh _____

6. epchse _____

7. rtnMsuohuRmeo _____

8. rarboelit _____

9. ctarGromEentipaa _____

10. MoclaienlnmoiLr _____

# Abraham Lincoln Word Search

```
E T V R O T A R E B I L L M F Q N N B
K G R E A T E M A N C I P A T O R O A
Z F J W L L B B L K H M B U N A E F G
Q N F W O W X U N H H R T S L E D L R
T M C Q R F J N W R A T H D J Z N N U
R T R I H Y B T G H N Q Z C J W A M B
E N K I V F Z B A E L G F K E D Y Z S
U D X D Y I E M D X P S H J T E X W Y
K M W X E Q L I V K M X Z G S V P M T
Y C X Q R I S W J R Q M L N Z Y L S T
E D P F N E J Q A O I N W L C U B O E
M Q P C R R X H S R A P K G X A H X G
P N O P N I T E U Q O L E T W H E H
D L I E R O M H S U R T N U O M O B U
N L A I R O M E M N L O C N I L G W S
```

## Word Bank

Abraham Lincoln

Civil War

eloquent

Gettysburg

Great Emancipator

liberator

Lincoln Memorial

Mount Rushmore

president

speech

# Abraham Lincoln Crossword

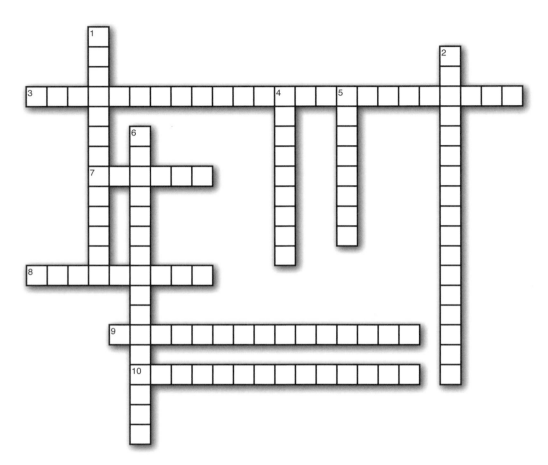

**Across**

3. U.S. declaration of freedom to all slaves
7. a formal address given to an audience
8. someone who sets a person or people free
9. monument dedicated to Abraham Lincoln's memory
10. signer of the Emancipation Proclamation

**Down**

1. famous presidential landmark in South Dakota
2. speech given in memory of the battle at Gettysburg
4. Abraham Lincoln was elected to this office in 1860
5. the war fought in America between the North and the South
6. nickname given to Abraham Lincoln

# Alexander Graham Bell

Samuel Morse sent the first telegraph message in 1844. This changed everything. For over 50 years the telegraph was the most important step forward in communication. In order to send a telegram, you would have to travel to the nearest telegraph office, which in some cases was many miles away. You would then write out your message, being careful to use the fewest amount of words possible, because each word was very costly. For these reasons, people only sent telegrams when absolutely necessary.

With the invention of the telephone came instant communication. Not ticks and dashes translated into letters, but simply using your voice. I imagine that at first people felt strange talking into a machine and then expecting a reply. Now, we don't think twice about it, but during Alexander Graham Bell's time it was borderline insanity.

Dr. Bell was an inventor, professor, and visionary. Born in 1847 in Edinburgh, Scotland, Aleck showed signs of a great mind when he was just a boy. He created his first successful invention at the age of nine. It was a machine that removed husks from grain. Aleck, as he was called, was taught at home by his mother until the age of eleven. Being almost completely deaf, she gave him more than just a basic home education. Eliza was an accomplished pianist despite her inability to hear. She passed her knowledge of the piano on to Aleck, along with a sense that just because something seems unlikely, that means little when compared to human innovation.

Bell's future was shaped by his childhood, beginning with his love for music. He understood the way instruments worked, and had the capacity to hear a piece of music and then play it perfectly right afterward. At one time, he thought about devoting his life to being a musician. Another aspect of his family life that left an impression on young Aleck was that two generations of elocution experts came before him. His grandfather was a professor of elocution, and his father created a system of visible speech that Aleck would later use to teach the Deaf how to speak. He was always fascinated with sounds and the vibrations of speech, seeing them in a way that no one else did.

In April of 1871, Bell moved to America. He had accepted a teaching position at the Boston School for the Deaf. Within just days, Aleck made a huge impact on the school. Using the knowledge his father had passed down to him, he was a very successful teacher. Next, he began tutoring Deaf children. This gave him more time to focus on his inventions. At the time, he was working on something he called the harmonic telegraph. It was the idea that if you used varying tones, you could send multiple messages along the same wire.

One of his students was Mabel Hubbard. She had lost her hearing at the age of four from scarlet fever. Although she was able to speak and read lips, her father hired Mr. Bell to make Mabel's speech even clearer. She was able to learn quickly, and didn't need Aleck's tutoring for long. The connection between them grew to much more than just tutor and student though. Aleck had found the partner of his life in Mabel. Always supportive, at times she believed in the telephone more than Aleck.

Think about the idea for just a moment, and pretend that you've never used or heard of a telephone before. Now think of the concept, talking through a wire. Does that sound a little crazy to you? It did to most people. It took a special kind of bravery to pursue such an extraordinary idea. Even after he proved that the invention worked, people thought it would never become common, that it was just a toy. So he proved them wrong again.

*Tele* means distance, or from afar. *Phon* means sound. Put them together, and *telephone* means sound from afar.

It was during his research for the harmonic telegraph that Aleck became obsessed with the question: could the human voice be transmitted through wire? One day, while working on the method of sending multiple telegraphs, Aleck and his assistant, Mr. Watson, happened upon a very important discovery. It was June 2, 1875, and Mr. Watson accidentally transmitted a twanging sound along a wire. It occurred when one of his instruments was stuck, and he plucked it with his finger. At the other end of the wire, Bell's trained ear heard a sound that was unlike anything he had ever heard before. With this, he knew instantly that if this sound could be transmitted, a human voice could too.

His idea for the telephone was possible. Experiments soon began. Alexander Graham Bell's mind was constantly turning. He moved fast, and thought even faster. Exploring his ideas, he devoted himself to his inventions, sacrificing everything, at times, even food. He and Watson lived together in a low-rent attic. What little money they had went to supplies. Often, Mr. Watson would be wakened in the middle of the night by an excited Bell who couldn't wait until morning to try out a new theory. It was after many attempts and much work that the first phrase was spoken clearly through the telephone on March 10th, 1876. A frantic Bell said, *"Mr. Watson, come here, I want you."* Calling to his friend, Aleck had just spilled acid on himself. Watson came running breathlessly in and told Bell that he had heard his words as clearly as if he were standing in the room. After that, Aleck cared little about the burning acid.

He had created two important inventions in one—the microphone and the loudspeaker. The microphone is a device that turns your voice's sound waves into an electrical signal. The signal then travels through a wire that is connected to the loud speaker. Finally, the loud speaker takes the electrical signal and converts it back into sound waves.

It would take a little time, and a lot more work before the telephone became acceptable to the public. Bell and Watson travelled to various cities making demonstrations of their invention. People began to see what the future could be. They thought of how much less complicated it would be to communicate with a friend, or call on the doctor. They felt safer knowing that it would only take a phone call for the fire department to dispatch help. Four years after the first phone call, over sixty thousand phones had been installed in America.

On January 25th of 1915, Alexander Graham Bell and Thomas Watson made history once again. A network of telephone lines had finally been built from one end of the country to the other. Using the familiar instrument before him, Aleck spoke from New York to his faithful assistant who was more than 3,000 miles away. With a clever wit, and a feeling of nostalgia, Bell used the same fateful words that had changed his life thirty-nine years before, *"Mr. Watson, come here, I want you."* Watson's reply: *"It will take me five days to get there now!"*

> *"Don't keep forever on the public road, going only where others have gone, and following one after the other like a flock of sheep. Leave the beaten track occasionally and dive into the woods."*

- Alexander Graham Bell

Mr. Bell did not stay on the public road. He did not follow others. He blazed his own trail, changing the world with his ideas. We thank you Dr. Bell, for the courage of your innovation. Because of your work, the door to communication has been opened wide.

## Timeline Activity

Put things in perspective. Place Alexander Graham Bell's figure on the timeline in the year 1876, which was when he spoke the first clear words on the telephone. Then identify two other events that happened in history during his life and add them to your timeline. You might also add a symbol or picture that represents this event.

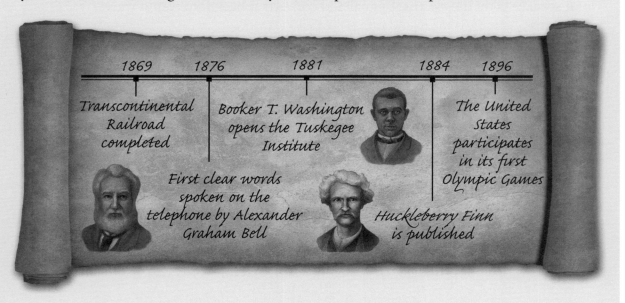

| 1869 | 1876 | 1881 | 1884 | 1896 |

Transcontinental Railroad completed

Booker T. Washington opens the Tuskegee Institute

The United States participates in its first Olympic Games

First clear words spoken on the telephone by Alexander Graham Bell

Huckleberry Finn is published

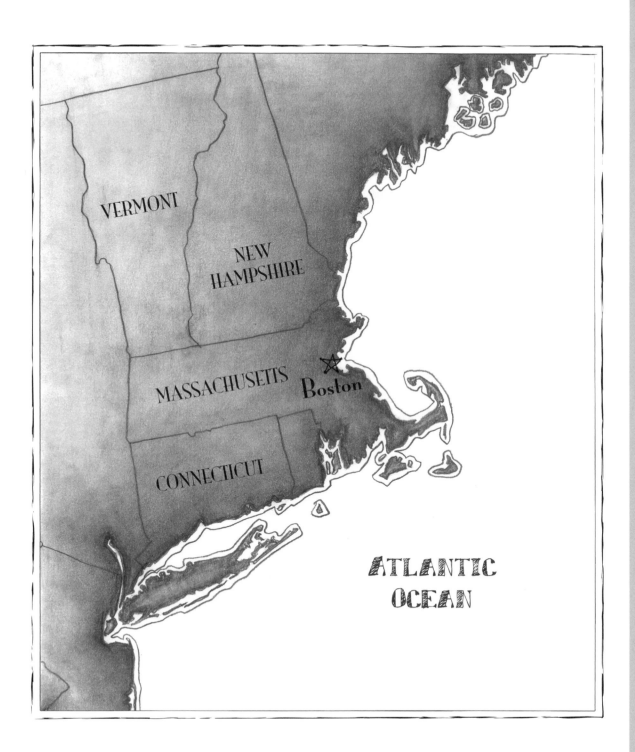

## Discussion

Alexander Graham Bell stood by his ideas even when the majority of people told him they would never work. They said that even if they did work they would never catch on. What do you think helped him to keep going? If you were in a similar situation, what do you think would give you the strength to carry on?

## Activity

The telephone changed the way people communicated. Talk with your family about the way you think cell phones have changed the way people live now. What does your family do differently because of cell phone use? Keep track of how often you and your family use the cell phone compared to how often you use your home phone for one day and then for one week. Do you think the need for home phones will change in the future?

## Wordscramble

Here is a list of scrambled words that relate to the profile you read about Alexander Graham Bell. Unscramble the letters and write the words correctly.

1. Stonaldc _____

2. aprelregmtociahhn _____

3. HbaebulrabMd _____

4. tsBoon _____

5. smTnaWsahtoo _____

6. eleohnetp _____

7. raaxnGeeBarmlldhAel _____

8. normecpioh _____

9. kepodalseur _____

10. etrnovni _____

# Using Context

Read the sentence and then look at the word in *italics*. Tell what you think that word means. Then look it up in a dictionary to confirm, or make sure of, the meaning. Tell someone about each word that you got correct. Remember, you will get better at understanding word meanings as you practice using context, or the words around a word.

1. Dr. Bell was an inventor, professor, and *visionary*. (paragraph 3)

   I think *visionary* means: _____

   Dictionary definition: _____

   My meaning was: (Circle one)   correct   had correct parts   not close

2. She passed her knowledge of the piano on to Aleck, along with a sense that just because something seems unlikely, that means little when compared to human *innovation*. (paragraph 3)

   I think *innovation* means: _____

   Dictionary definition: _____

   My meaning was: (Circle one)   correct   had correct parts   not close

3. With this, he knew instantly that if this sound could be *transmitted*, a human voice could too. (paragraph 9)

   I think *transmitted* means: _____

   Dictionary definition: _____

   My meaning was: (Circle one)   correct   had correct parts   not close

# Alexander Graham Bell Word Search

```
J Y M L U F V V J H H C N Z L Z F T A
Z M V Y Q D W C G U M W X E T E L H L
D Z I N V E N T O R U C R D D K J O E
N R G C P G X L O V B V K L H N F M X
V R A Q R Q N W D C L F Q O O W V A A
D S S B E O D O X W I Z H U Y I F S N
V T C U B S P I X S U I M D A N E W D
L J V O S U C H I Z T C R S J E U A E
O B G Z T R H D O E N O H P E L E T R
K O S C L L B L O N T F N E M A M S G
X S O L N B A K E L E Y W A I F A O B
X T I W H M M N N B R T T K D Y N N E
T O D F S D L T D S A G W E L T O L L
C N J T L Z X B M W A M F R P U R T L
H P A R G E L E T C I N O M R A H I E
```

## Word Bank

Alexander G. Bell

Boston

harmonic telegraph

inventor

loud speaker

Mabel Hubbard

microphone

Scotland

telephone

Thomas Watson

# Alexander Graham Bell Crossword

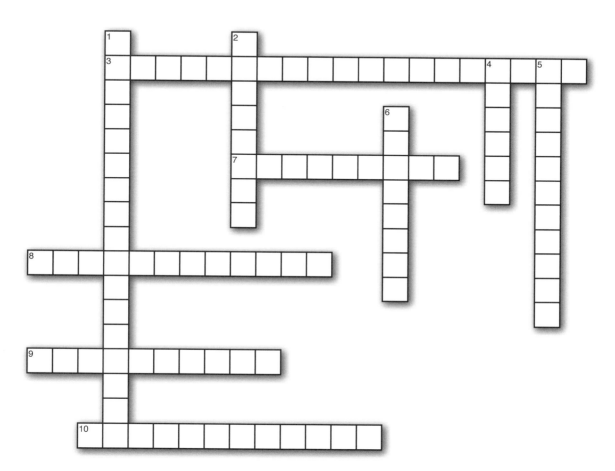

## Across

3. inventor of the telephone
7. name of invention that allows speech to travel through a wire
8. wife of Alexander Graham Bell
9. instrument that turns sound waves into electrical impulses
10. Alexander Graham Bell's assistant

## Down

1. concept by Alexander Graham Bell of using multiple telegraphs
2. what a person is called when he comes up with new ideas for making or doing things
4. the capitol of Massachusetts
5. instrument that enables electrical impulses to be translated into sound
6. home country of Alexander Graham Bell

# Henry Ford

*"I will build a motor car for the great multitude ... it will be so low in price that no man making a good salary will be unable to own one and enjoy with his family the blessing of hours of pleasure in God's great open spaces."*

- Henry Ford

From the time he was little, Henry Ford liked taking things apart. He wanted to see how they worked, and he wasn't always able to put them back together. To him, though, it was worth it. Never very interested in anything else, Henry was born to be an engineer. His father was a farmer, and he always thought that his oldest son, Henry, would take over for him one day. He soon realized that Henry had a bigger future.

Born in Michigan in the year 1863, Henry Ford grew up in the early days of the Industrial Revolution. Little did he realize at the time, but he would be one of the major influences in this movement. When he was sixteen, Ford left his home to move to Detroit. There he worked as an apprentice machinist for three years. Working with his hands, he gained a deeper knowledge and appreciation for the way things work.

Following his years as an apprentice, Ford was hired by the Westinghouse company to work with steam engines. His wife, Clara, was always supportive of her husband's experiments and even used to help him with them when needed. Ford later became the chief engineer for the Edison Illuminating Company. With this position, he finally had enough income to invest in some of his own ideas. During this time, he created his first self-propelled vehicle. It was called the Ford Quadricycle. A crude first attempt, it was a stepping stone toward his later success.

At a meeting of executives for the Edison Illuminating Company, Henry Ford made an acquaintance that gave him an important push in the right direction. One of his heroes, Thomas Edison, found out that Ford was working on a gas-powered car. Upon hearing this, he asked Ford a series of questions, and with a bang of his hand on the table told him, *"Young man, that's the thing! You have it!"* This gave Ford the courage he needed to continue taking strides toward his goal. Later, Ford reflected on Edison's words saying, *"No man up to then had given me any encouragement. I had hoped that I was headed right. Sometimes I knew that I was, sometimes I only wondered, but here, all at once and out of a clear sky, the greatest inventive genius in the world had given me complete approval."* A friendship was made that day that would last the rest of their lives. Ford even built a museum in honor of his friend, called the Edison Institute. It was dedicated on the fiftieth anniversary of the light bulb.

Following Edison's encouragement, Ford left the Illuminating Company and went through a trial and error process of starting his own company. Two failed attempts later, The Ford Motor Company was born. The definition of revolutionary is: involving or causing a complete or dramatic change. Henry Ford revolutionized America. Because of his Model T, which debuted in 1908, the average American was no longer so restricted in how far he could travel, or how long it would take him. The possibilities seemed endless for the person who traded in a horse and buggy for a Model T.

Up until Henry Ford, cars were only toys that the wealthy got to play with. They were made by hand, and had a reputation for being very unreliable. The problem was that there was no system.

So Henry Ford created a system for mass production. It was called the assembly line. Instead of a few people spending hours to build each car, there was a line of people who only had to learn one job. They didn't need to become apprentices for years like Henry had. Each one only needed to master one thing, and do it over and over again. Their jobs needed to be done exactly the same way every time. This created a system that was not only efficient, but produced parts that were uniform. It would revolutionize the automobile industry and the way things were made all around the world. Due to the exceedingly reduced amount of time it took to build each car, the cost could be lowered to the point of affordability.

Henry Ford had a vision, and he knew it was possible to solve the problems he saw. His vision was a car that was affordable, reliable, and easy to fix. So he worked as long and as hard as he needed to, to make this dream come true. It was possible. This is the truth that every revolutionary must hold onto. There is a way. All a person has to do is find it.

*"Failure is simply an opportunity to begin again, this time more intelligently."*

- Henry Ford

In another revolutionary move, Henry Ford raised the average pay of his workers to five dollars an hour, doubling the standard wages of his time. And not only did he raise his workers' pay, he lessened their hours. The result was workers who took pride in their jobs. Feeling valued, they worked hard and produced quality workmanship. Needless to say, Henry Ford never lacked in people wanting jobs.

Using his corporation for good during World War II, Ford lent his vast resources to the war effort. Building B-24 Bombers, jeeps, and tanks, Ford's company was a part of what Franklin Roosevelt called the Arsenal of Democracy. Ford and his family also spent time investing in their community. They devoted funds to charitable organizations, and even created one of their own which still exists today called the Ford Foundation.

*"Enthusiasm is the yeast that makes your hopes shine to the stars. Enthusiasm is the sparkle in your eyes, the swing in your gait. The grip of your hand, the irresistible surge of will and energy to execute your ideas."*

- Henry Ford

Henry Ford changed the way Americans lived and traveled. His choices were not always worthy of admiration, but we can learn from his tenacity and his determination. The Model T was the first dependable and affordable car in our history. It was Henry's dream, and he wasn't willing to stop until it became a reality. After almost twenty years on the market, the last Model T was built in 1927. By then, more than fifteen million of them had been sold. Henry Ford believed that he could change the world, and he did.

## Discussion

Henry Ford had a vision to make an affordable, reliable automobile. In order for this to be a reality, he had to make changes in the way cars were made. This change made cars easier for everyone to buy. Is there something you think should be easier for everyone to have? Think of ways to increase everyone's ability to have that thing. What changes would need to be made in the way things are done for that to happen?

## Timeline Activity

Put things in perspective. Place Henry Ford's figure on the timeline in the year 1908, which was when his Model T revolutionized American travel. Then identify two other events that happened in history during his life and add them to your timeline. You might also add a symbol or picture that represents this event.

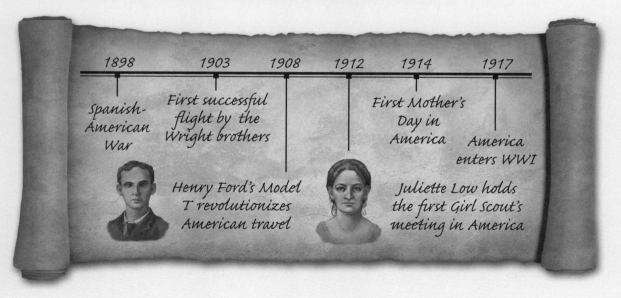

1898 — Spanish-American War

1903 — First successful flight by the Wright brothers

1908 — Henry Ford's Model T revolutionizes American travel

1912 — Juliette Low holds the first Girl Scout's meeting in America

1914 — First Mother's Day in America

1917 — America enters WWI

## Activity

This week, keep track of how much your family drives, keeping a log of the mileage used. At the end of the week, add it all up. Are you surprised at how much you travel? Choose a place that you go on a regular basis and calculate how many miles it is from your home. If a horse and buggy travelled at about five miles per hour, how long would it take you to get to the place you've chosen using this method? Do you think this would change how often you travel and where you go?

## True or False

Create five true or false statements about this story. Present them to your family members. Mix up the true and false statements to keep everyone thinking. Be sure sure to make up an answer key so that your readers will know when they are correct. To see a sample True or False, turn to page 203.

## Wordscramble

Here is a list of scrambled words that relate to the profile you read about Henry Ford. Unscramble the letters and write the words correctly.

1. nvietoinn _____

2. rFneHrdoy _____

3. odtoaomFoMyCrrpn _____

4. ossnihTdaoEm _____

5. ivnntinoao _____

6. aymislebnsel _____

7. eTdMlo _____

8. oneprei _____

9. crgsaa _____

10. ngMaichi _____

## Write a Letter

If you could speak to Henry Ford, what would you say? Would you tell him how grateful you are for his sacrifices? Or maybe you would ask him questions about what it was like to do what he did. Write a letter or an email to Henry Ford. You can also make a postcard instead of writing a letter or email. On your postcard, create a scene that represents the person you read about. Include at least one quote that you think represents this person well.

# Henry Ford Word Search

```
F Y N A P M O C R O T O M D R O F F Y
L I C S L V A M Z F S D T B D X C A S
C R L S W Y C P O I X X G B X D I I N
B Y H E J R U K O W N Z L R A P N L L
T H O M A S E D I S O N M A B N V L T
F E H B G Y T E S U A X K C O L E H W
X N L L D W Q X N H M E R V W U N D Q
H R A Y M V H R G O Y I A T J P T E M
N Y O L A S Z F M Q I T C X N V I X D
Q F W I G I B V S O I P S H P Y O E G
R O Z N W W Y S K O D F A Z I S N K X
A R Y E F M K P N Z Z E G W I G E C T
C D C X K J G Y G I G G L O U N A Z K
N H T I D P O X V Q B E D T R R G N G
G U S O Z V A V K S L B L T J U O G N
```

## Word Bank

| | |
|---|---|
| assembly line | invention |
| Ford Motor Company | Michigan |
| gas car | Model T |
| Henry Ford | pioneer |
| innovation | Thomas Edison |

# Henry Ford Crossword

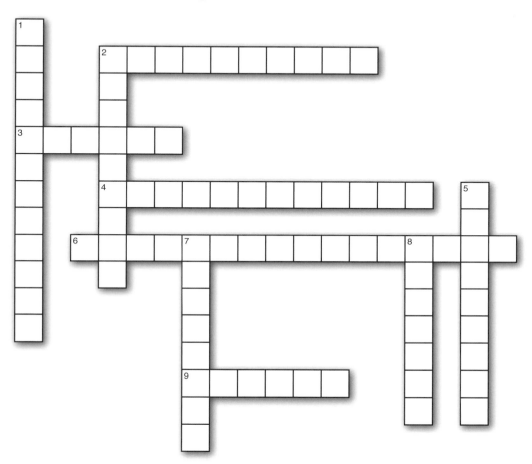

## Across

2. the process of coming up with new ideas
3. first affordable car in America
4. inventor of the lightbulb
6. company started by Henry Ford
9. a car that is powered by gasoline

## Down

1. a line of people each adding a different piece in order to build a thing
2. what something is called when someone discovers a way to make it for the first time
5. creator of the Model T
7. the home state of Henry Ford
8. a person who goes before others blazing a new trail

# *Alvin C. York*

On April 2nd of 1917, Woodrow Wilson asked Congress for an official declaration of war. The United States was set to enter World War I.

The world had never seen such destruction. World War I marked the first time in history that things like chemical warfare were used in combat. The advancements that had been made in technology to better society also raised the number of casualties war could produce. War is filled with stories of loss and heartache. So when something miraculous happens, it becomes a great light in the darkness. Such is the story of Sergeant York.

Alvin C. York grew up in the backwoods of the Tennessee mountains. He was born in the year 1887 in a small town called Pall Mall. He never had much time for school as there were always chores to do, but his father taught him a great deal about being a man. He showed him how to till a field, to hunt, and how to shoot a rifle with accuracy. Alvin was later regarded as one of the best marksmen Fentress County had ever seen. This was no small feat in a town of men who were each skilled with a rifle. Alvin's father instilled other things in him too. He taught him to be fearless, to be true, and to care for his family. Alvin would apply these lessons of virtue later on in his life.

He was a man of simplicity. He was hard-working, with few plans for himself except to live the life his father had taught him about. His dreams were to marry a young girl by the name of Gracie Williams, to own his own house and his own fields. He never dreamed of becoming a world-famous hero.

On June 5th, 1917, Alvin York received a notice to register for the draft. It was hard for him and others in the town to understand why a war being fought so far away could require their help. Most people in secluded towns like Pall Mall didn't even know why they were fighting. They didn't realize that if given the chance, Germany would take over the whole world, not just Europe.

York went through basic training at Camp Gordon in Georgia. He proved to be an expert shot, a strong laborer, and a natural leader. It was the morning of October 8th, 1918, when Alvin York's courage would be truly tested. He was very far from home, among the trees of the Argonne Forest in France. York, who had been promoted to corporal, and seventeen other men set out on a mission to overthrow a German stronghold and return with prisoners.

At first, it seemed as though everything would go as planned. They had captured a number of Germans without much resistance, but in a flash, everything changed. Enemy machine gunners located at the top of the hill who were engaged in combat on the other side, caught word of the Americans behind them. They quickly readjusted their weapons to face the men. As if by signal, the German prisoners being held all laid flat, and a torrential rain of bullets fell on the Americans.

One of the greatest abilities York possessed was keeping calm under pressure. At the onset of the bullets, he had been on the left end of his group. It was a position he could maneuver in. The other survivors were pinned to the ground, unable to take action or leave their prisoners. It was up to one man from the mountains of Tennessee to do what he could. So York waited for an opportunity, and finally there was a lull in the bullets. German soldiers, thinking that they had killed or wounded any threats, began coming out to see the results of the battle. York took his opportunity. With stealth and a quickness that could have only come from his days in the woods, he began taking out the enemy. Alvin had been taught to look for the most minute movements while hunting at home. He learned to notice the falling of a leaf, the changing of a shadow, and the tip of a tail as he stalked his prey. Now, instead of hunting animals, York used his training to defeat German soldiers. His uncanny accuracy and carefully placed bullets wouldn't allow him to miss a shot. He couldn't miss a shot if he wanted to survive and save his men.

A group of six German soldiers noticed that York was on his own, and since shooting at him from a distance was proving futile, they charged with fixed bayonets. For most men, the battle would have been over right then and there, because Alvin had no shots left in his rifle. Fearless and collected he pulled out his pistol, and one by one, from the back of the group to the front, Alvin eliminated the threat. While staying concealed, he was continually yelling for the Germans to give up so that no more lives would be lost. At first, they thought this arrogant American was a fool. But as he persisted, they could not stop him. Finally, the unthinkable happened—surrender! One man almost single-handedly brought down a battalion of German machine gunners.

Always keeping his composure, York began to organize his prisoners. Only eight Americans had survived the assault uninjured. Together, the men, with York at the front, eventually led 132 German prisoners into captivity.

It was a story so incredible that it had to be thoroughly investigated and verified before anyone could believe it. Each American soldier who had seen it with his own eyes confirmed the same story. Alvin York was a hero.

Upon hearing about York's bravery, Major General C.P. Summerall praised him in front of his division with these words:

> *"It is an honor to command such soldiers as you. Your conduct reflects great credit not only upon the American army, but upon the American people. Your deeds will be recorded in the history of this great war and they will live as an inspiration not only to your comrades but to the generations that will come after us."*

The hill where the famous battle occurred has since been renamed York's Hill. His story travelled throughout the troops, across countries, and across the ocean. The newspapers of America had a new hero to introduce to the country. They welcomed him like no other. He became one of the most decorated American soldiers of World War I.

Alvin York was promoted to Sergeant and received many awards and countless receptions. General John J. Pershing considered him to be the greatest civilian soldier of the war, and presented him with the most rare and esteemed Congressional Medal of Honor. Supreme Allied Commander, Marshal Foch, awarded York with France's medal for honor, the Croix de Guerre. He stated, *"What York did was the greatest thing accomplished by any soldier of all the armies of Europe."*

When he returned to the United States, York received a hero's welcome many times over. A parade was thrown in his honor, as well as a banquet, when he first arrived in New York City. From there, he visited Washington D.C., where the House of Representatives gave him a standing ovation.

While he was ever grateful and humbled by the attention, Sergeant York couldn't help but think of the home he missed so much. He thought of his sweet Gracie, who he fully intended to marry as soon as he got back; his mother, who had given him the strength of character to do what he did; and the woods that called to him to return. In his mind, he still had at least a couple more years of work before he could provide a house to share with Gracie. He would later find out that the Nashville Rotary Club purchased a 400-acre farm for him. His life with Gracie could finally begin.

Sergeant York used his new-found fame for good. He formed the Alvin C. York Foundation to better the education opportunities for children in his region. When World War II came around, York, ever ready to serve his country, tried to enlist. He was denied however, because of his age and his health. So he did what he could, traveling the country in support of the war effort and raising money for charities like the Red Cross. When York finally let the story of his life be made into a movie in 1941, it received eleven Oscar nominations and was the highest-grossing movie of that year. He put all the income toward building a school in his hometown.

Alvin York died in the year 1964 as a devoted husband to his lifelong love Gracie, an admired father to their eight children, and one of the truest American heroes this country has seen.

> *"Courage is not simply one of the virtues, but the form of every virtue at the testing point."*

> - C.S. Lewis

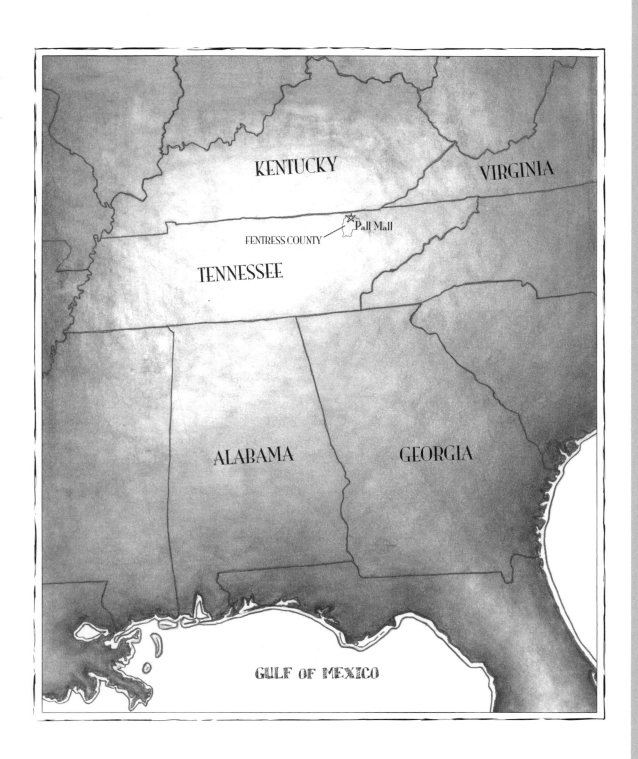

## Discussion

Sergeant York demonstrated bravery and clear thinking that surprised even him. Can you think of a time when you surprised yourself with quick thinking or bravery? What character qualities do you think enabled Sergeant York to act quickly and confidently? Humility was one of his greatest strengths. How do you think someone can gain this character trait?

## Timeline Activity

Put things in perspective. Place Alvin C. York's figure on the timeline in the year 1918, which was when he defeated a battalion of Machine gunners. Then identify two other events that happened in history during his life and add them to your timeline. You might also add a symbol or picture that represents this event.

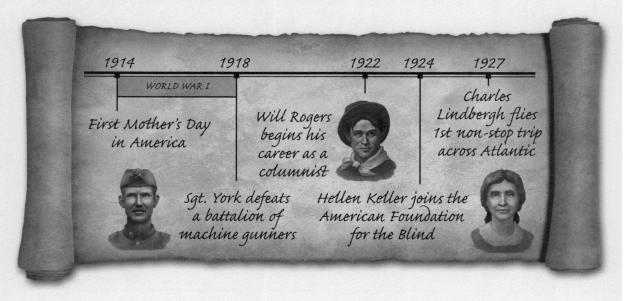

1914     1918     1922   1924   1927

WORLD WAR I

First Mother's Day in America

Will Rogers begins his career as a columnist

Sgt. York defeats a battalion of machine gunners

Hellen Keller joins the American Foundation for the Blind

Charles Lindbergh flies 1st non-stop trip across Atlantic

## Activity

Sergeant York received the highest military decoration available, the Congressional Medal of Honor. Learn more about this symbol of bravery. When is it awarded?

Talk with your parents about watching the movie based on Alvin York's life called *Sergeant York*.

## True or False

Create five true or false statements about this story. Present them to your family members. Mix up the true and false statements to keep everyone thinking. Be sure sure to make up an answer key so that your readers will know when they are correct. To see a sample True or False, turn to page 203.

## Wordscramble

Here is a list of scrambled words that relate to the profile you read about Alvin C. York. Unscramble the letters and write the words correctly.

1. anretsge _____

2. laalPlMl _____

3. orWrIaWdl _____

4. rGpmodaoCn _____

5. aamlGsiieiWrcl _____

6. nAooserenrFgt _____

7. ecFarn _____

8. rfoMdHnaeool _____

9. oCkYAlnirv _____

10. nmmsaark _____

## Using Context

Read the sentence and then look at the word in *italics*. Tell what you think that word means. Then look it up in a dictionary to confirm, or make sure of, the meaning. Tell someone about each word that you got correct. Remember, you will get better at understanding word meanings as you practice using context, or the words around a word.

1. Alvin would apply these lessons of *virtue* later on in his life. (paragraph 3)

    I think *virtue* means: _____

    Dictionary definition: _____

    My meaning was: (Circle one)　　correct　　had correct parts　　not close

2. At the onset of the bullets, he had been on the left end of his group. It was a position he could *maneuver* in. (paragraph 8)

    I think *maneuver* means: _____

    Dictionary definition: _____

    My meaning was: (Circle one)　　correct　　had correct parts　　not close

3. His *uncanny* accuracy and carefully placed bullets wouldn't allow him to miss a shot. (paragraph 8)

    I think *uncanny* means: _____

    Dictionary definition: _____

    My meaning was: (Circle one)　　correct　　had correct parts　　not close

# Alvin C. York Word Search

```
Z K R O Y C N I V L A O L L H S X E G
C O E Z X C S O A T W R G L V I E O R
T P W X B G F K M X O D L A N X Y X A
C M S B B A R P L N R C T M O G H V C
D M L F U W Q R O Y L W R L D G X W I
R R F O Y U O H W Y D O P L R D A G E
R E H H X T F L J W H O A O Y W X W
B X J V K O N K C W A G Z P G J U V I
I Q N V L E V A E V R Q N A P L X C L
C X J A C C E M E Q I O U U M J Y H L
V G D D D N N L B G R C W W A D S F I
R E O O J A D D A E R R F R C L R T A
M A U N W R D K Z Z A E J F D C K V M
V P W F Z F W X X N A M S K R A M C S
K A R G O N N E F O R E S T O Z I C M
```

## Word Bank

| | |
|---|---|
| Alvin C. York | marksman |
| Argonne Forest | Medal of Honor |
| Camp Gordon | Pall Mall |
| France | sergeant |
| Gracie Williams | World War I |

# Alvin C. York Crossword

## Across

4. famous hero of World War I
6. small town in Tennessee where Alvin York was born
7. the highest military decoration
9. the military rank given to Alvin York
10. a person who is precise in shooting

## Down

1. Alvin York's wife
2. military training camp in Georgia
3. a war also known as the Great War
5. forest in France where York's Hill is located
8. country located directly across the English Channel from England

# Hellen Keller

Helen Keller was born a healthy baby in Tuscumbia, Alabama, on June 27th, 1880. She was a bright and cheerful toddler. Soon she began spouting out words, and learned to walk on her first birthday. But when Helen was nineteen months old tragedy struck. She came down with an extremely high fever. The doctors feared she wouldn't survive, but then she began to recover. Her family didn't know it yet, but the illness would quickly steal her ability to see and hear.

It was a fateful thing. For many people, deafness and blindness are from birth, but Helen had seen the world and heard her parents' voices. To then go to a world of isolation at such a young age must have been terrifying.

Extremely brave and intelligent, she learned how to keep living her life despite the challenges. Anyone put in such a position would be tempted to simply retreat, but not Helen. It is because of this fire inside of her that she changed the way deaf and blind people were perceived.

By the time Helen reached the age of six, she was growing more and more frustrated with her inability to communicate. She had so many questions and curiosities. She had even made up sixty different signs that she could use with her family members. Still, this wasn't enough. Helen needed more. Though they weren't quite sure what to do, her parents started looking for opportunities. They took her to see an eye doctor who, unfortunately, could do nothing for Helen's eyes, but he did suggest that they visit Alexander Graham Bell. Dr. Bell, inventor of the telephone, would be a lifelong friend of Helen's. Both his mother and his wife were deaf, and he had some connections that opened doors for Helen's education. He was the one who suggested that Helen's mother contact the Perkins Institution for the Blind.

Anne Sullivan had just graduated valedictorian of her class from Perkins when she accepted the teaching position for the young Helen Keller. Little did she know that this decision would define the rest of her life, as well as Helen's. When Anne was only five, she contracted a disease that left her half blind. Later, she would be able to have an operation that restored most of her sight. At eight, her mother died, and her father was unfit to care for her. At the age of ten, she was sent to live at the state poorhouse. Always asking people to read to her, Anne had a deep desire to learn. She went to the Perkins Institution for the Blind when she was fourteen. Putting her childhood tragedies behind her, Anne let nothing hold her back. A feisty and spirited young woman, she was the perfect match for Helen.

Helen later referred to the day Anne arrived in 1887 as her soul's birthday. Not only did Anne teach Helen how to communicate, but she tamed her temperament by enforcing manners and respectful behavior. After about a month of Anne's patient instruction, Helen finally connected the word Anne had spelled into her hand, w-a-t-e-r, to the actual flowing substance running over her skin. That day, Helen learned thirty new words. Her mind devoured the information Anne gave her. Using unconventional methods, Teacher, as Helen referred to her, often took Helen outside, signing and discovering the world around them. Within four months Helen had learned four hundred words. She also learned to write. Helen could write in Braille and would even use a ruler as a guide to draw letters.

From there, she set her sights on a formal education. First, Helen went with Anne to her alma mater, the Perkins Institution, in Boston. There she focused on refining her communication skills. She learned to read lips through touch and to read Braille. She learned the use of a Braille typewriter, as well as a conventional one. Ready for the next challenge, she attended the Wright-Humason School for the Deaf, where she began learning how to speak. Next, to prepare for college, Helen went to the Cambridge School for Young Ladies. Lastly, she graduated, cum laude, from Radcliffe College in 1904. Radcliffe was the sister college of Harvard University, and one of the best schools in the country for women. Helen was the first deaf and blind person to receive a college degree.

What an achievement! Helen became a symbol of hope for all those like her. She proved that no matter the circumstances, almost anything is possible. Don't deceive yourself into thinking that it was an easy thing she did. Most books at her time were not available in Braille. This meant that Anne was at her side at all times, spelling out each word into her hand. It was hard work for both women. Because of Helen's strength and determination, and Anne's faithful help, she was able to endure.

> *"Self-pity is our worst enemy and if we yield to it, we can never do anything wise in this world."*
>
> - Helen Keller

Just before her graduation year, at the age of twenty-two, Helen published her first book. Named *The Story of My Life*, she dedicated it to her good friend Alexander Graham Bell. Helen wanted others to be able to learn from her struggles and her triumphs. *The Story of My Life* has since been translated into fifty different languages.

After graduating, Helen and Anne put together a Vaudeville act to try and bring in some money. During the act, Anne would tell about the teaching methods she used, and Helen would then give a short inspirational message and answer questions. In some of her answers, you got to see Helen's playful side. Here are a few examples:

Question: *What is your age?*
Answer: *Between sixteen and sixty.*

Question: *Do you desire your sight more than anything?*
Answer: *No! No! I would rather walk with a friend in the dark, than walk alone in the light.*

Question: *What is the greatest affliction—deafness, dumbness, or blindness?*
Answer: *Boneheadedness.*

In 1924, Helen teamed up with the American Foundation for the Blind, headquartered in New York City. She would represent and work for the AFB for 44 years. During the World Wars, Helen did what she could to aid the many wounded veterans who returned home. Traveling around the country, she sought to instill hope and encourage those with newly acquired disabilities. She especially spent time with veterans returning with vision impairments.

Helen went before Congress in Washington D.C. and encouraged them to support a bill that would devote $75,000 for Braille books. The bill passed. In 1964, she was awarded the Presidential Medal of Freedom by President Lyndon B. Johnson. The following year she was elected into the National Women's Hall of Fame. She was also the first woman to receive an honorary doctorate from Harvard University.

Helen Keller became an international symbol for overcoming adversity. Everyone who met her couldn't help but love her. Among her admirers were the likes of Mark Twain, Charlie Chaplin, Henry Ford, and of course the famous Dr. Bell. She lived the type of full life that most people only dream of. She travelled to thirty-nine different countries, met every U.S. president in her lifetime, and had the satisfaction of knowing that her efforts made a difference. Not many people could boast the same. Helen showed us that preconceived notions were outdated, and life was too short not to live it with a sense of humor and a purpose that you could be proud of. In her own words:

*"Life is either a great adventure or nothing."*

## Discussion

What would you do differently to communicate with a person who doesn't hear? How would you let a person who doesn't see know you're there? It was many years before anyone who was deaf and blind graduated from college like Hellen Keller had. Why do you think that is? What kind of personality trait would you need to accomplish something like this?

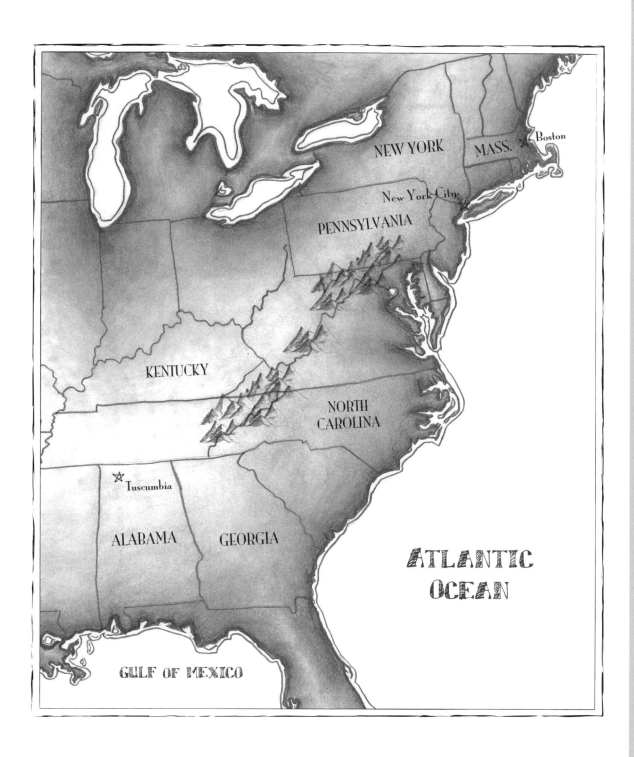

# Timeline Activity

Put things in perspective. Place Hellen Keller's figure on the timeline in the year 1924, which was when she joined the American Foundation for the Blind. Then identify two other events that happened in history during his life and add them to your timeline. You might also add a symbol or picture that represents this event.

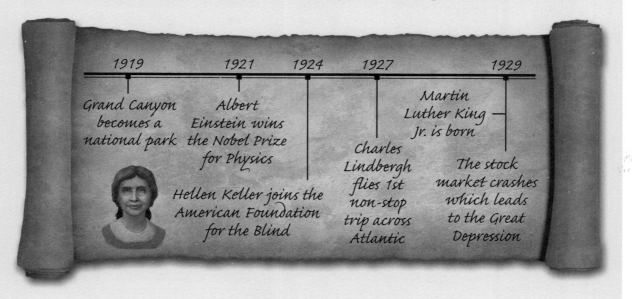

| 1919 | 1921 | 1924 | 1927 | 1929 |

Grand Canyon becomes a national park

Albert Einstein wins the Nobel Prize for Physics

Hellen Keller joins the American Foundation for the Blind

Charles Lindbergh flies 1st non-stop trip across Atlantic

Martin Luther King Jr. is born

The stock market crashes which leads to the Great Depression

# Activity

Find out how to make the letters of the Braille alphabet. Learn how to write your name in Braille. See if your local library carries *The Story of my Life* by Hellen Keller. Take the opportunity to read Hellen's life through her own eyes.

## Wordscramble

Here is a list of scrambled words that relate to the profile you read about Hellen Keller. Unscramble the letters and write the words correctly.

1. ellriBa _____

2. lKeellerenHl _____

3. ndrepglaii _____

4. sntsotrePInikiitnu _____

5. tume _____

6. uaedclum _____

7. lRigeedlffceoalC _____

8. lelvVudeai _____

9. abuimsTcu _____

10. uaneinSvllnA _____

## Write an Obituary

Write an obituary or a brief article that would appear about this person upon their passing. Since space is limited in a newspaper you may only use forty to forty-five words to describe this person. With such limited space, focus on the main events in their life. To see a sample obituary, turn to page 203.

# Hellen Keller Word Search

```
I J E G E L L O C E F F I L C D A R C
U X X S E Y D V K H C J G C P C W J E
D I W R E L L E K N E L L E H A L K V
Q P M N E D L Y X F F S Q T H O I V B
S A W I R U L I I K A H M W U Y P C K
H M I Z D X B S V Q W W C A O W R I D
M P B B R A I L L E H L X I U D E L M
B V Y V M T G S P H D U U H J F A V Z
O P I P M U T E C U X U Q M C E D Q H
W V C U N N C Q A C F G A P X Y I J B
N A V I L L U S E N N A M V Y E N V W
H T F X U X H C U M L A U D E W G I B
Q U L Z N S W P H T U Q T V E X Y S J
B Q O B Z L N S Z I Z C C C W F H J Z
P E R K I N S I N S T I T U T I O N M
```

## Word Bank

Anne Sullivan

Braille

cum laude

Hellen Keller

lip reading

mute

Perkins Institution

Radcliffe College

Tuscumbia

Vaudeville

# Hellen Keller Crossword

## Across

3. Latin term for graduating from college with distinction
5. prominent school for the blind in Boston
7. a variety show from the 1880s to the 1920s
9. Hellen Keller's teacher
10. sister college of Harvard University

## Down

1. birthplace of Hellen Keller
2. the state of being unable to speak
4. the practice of understanding words spoken by watching the mouth
6. famous deaf and blind woman
8. form of language using raised dots made for the blind

# *Irena Sendler*

Europe became a battleground of good versus evil during the disastrous years of World War II. There were many who chose to rise up against the injustices they witnessed. People found ways large and small to help in the resistance to Nazi Germany. Some opened their homes to refugees, others delivered messages, and still others posed as the opposition to gain inside information. One woman risked her life on a daily basis to save the most innocent and helpless of the Nazis' victims, Jewish children.

Irena Sendler grew up in a suburb of Warsaw, Poland, called Otwock. She was born in the year 1910. Her father, a doctor who mainly helped poor Jewish families in the community, taught Irena to always extend help to those in need. An only child, she took her father's example of sacrifice and kindness to heart.

She was twenty-nine years old when the Nazis began World War II with the invasion of Poland. Poland, which contained the largest Jewish population in Europe, would remain under German control until January of 1945. Some 450,000 Jews were forced into a sixteen-block ghetto in Warsaw. Because of the poor living conditions, it became notorious for disease and starvation. Almost as soon as it happened, Irena began to help by offering food and other support.

It was soon apparent that the ultimate goal of the Germans was to extinguish the residents inside the Warsaw Ghetto. Realizing this, Irena set out to rescue as many Jewish children from that fate as possible. She worked with a Polish underground organization named Zegota. Irena, knowing full well that if caught the sentence would be death, was put in charge of their children's division.

The most difficult and heart-wrenching part of Irena's job was convincing parents to let their children go. She could not guarantee their safety but she could guarantee that if they stayed, they would most likely perish. Although she was saving their lives, it still must have felt like she was tearing children away from their parents. Irena did her best to console the families. Mothers, fathers, and grandparents knew it was the best thing they could do for their precious loved ones, but that did not make saying goodbye any easier. For many, it was the final realization that escape was not probable. These extremely brave parents chose to put their babies in the hands of a stranger, and could only hope for their children's (and their own) survival.

Children were smuggled out in sacks, coffins, hiding under a stretcher in an ambulance, or through an underground passage. They would then be given new identities and taken to convents, orphanages, hospitals, and homes of families who were willing to offer shelter.

Irena painstakingly kept a list of all the children who were smuggled to freedom—their real names, and where they were sent. She decided that one day she would reunite them with whatever family members could be found. Irena placed this all-important list inside a jar, which she buried in a neighbor's yard. It had to be kept in the utmost secrecy. If found, Irena knew that every child, and those who helped in the escape, would be in grave danger.

In 1943, Irena's efforts were discovered. After her home was thoroughly searched by the Gestapo, she was taken to the Pawaik prison. While there, she encountered Nazi brutality first hand. For three months, they tried to force her to tell them with whom she was working. But Irena's bravery would only be made clearer by their torment. Under no circumstances would she give up what she knew. After she was sentenced to death, Zegota bribed a guard for Irena's release. Although the scars of the experience could not be erased, Irena was thankfully spared.

Following her time in the notorious Pawaik Prison, Sendler carried on the work that had cost her so much, only now it was under a different name. She refused to let the cruelty she faced keep her from continuing. When the war was finally over in 1945, Irena Sendler and her team were responsible for saving some 2,500 children. Using the list she had worked so hard to protect, Irena then set about reuniting as many children with their families as possible.

In later years, Irena watched as the world began to forget about the horrors of the Holocaust. But she never forgot the faces of the Jewish children she rescued, or their crying mothers who gave them to her. It was more than fifty years after her courageous acts before Irena was truly recognized for her efforts. Four girls from a high school in Kansas wrote a play about her incredible story, called *Life in a Jar*. Because of this play the world now knows her name. Such a story, once heard, spread quickly from one amazed person to the next. Now, thousands of websites, a book, and a movie are dedicated to her memory.

Irena was awarded Poland's highest civilian decoration, the Order of the White Eagle. She has been made an honorary citizen of Israel and was also nominated for the Nobel Peace Prize in 2007. After her picture began to circulate, Irena started receiving phone calls of thanks from those who recognized her. Elzbieta Ficowska, who was saved as a baby, stated, "Mrs. Sendler saved not only us, but also our children and grandchildren and the generations to come."

Some people found fame for their acts of service while others lived in obscurity. It was not until very recently that Irena Sendler gained the admiration she deserves. I wonder how many others there were like her, whose stories have never become known. Irena Sendler never saw herself as a hero. In fact, even to her death at the age of 98 she still maintained, "I could have done more."

## Discussion

"Mrs. Sendler saved not only us, but also our children and grandchildren and the generations to come." This quote, from one of the people saved by Irena, reminds us of the many lives affected by her efforts. Talk with your parents, and the oldest members of your family, about your family's history. Create a family tree from what you learn.

## Timeline Activity

Put things in perspective. Place Irena Sendler's figure on the timeline in the year 1939, which was when she began assisting the Jews of the Warsaw Ghetto. Then identify two other events that happened in history during his life and add them to your timeline. You might also add a symbol or picture that represents this event.

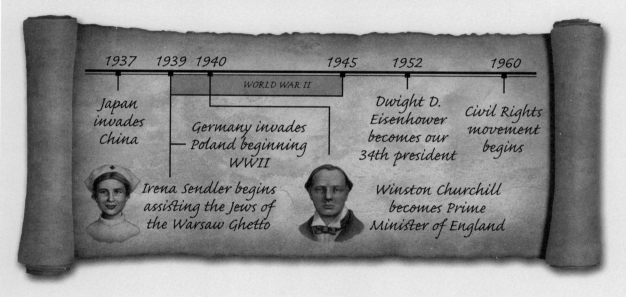

## Activity

Research the play that catapulted Irena Sendler's story into worldwide fame, a *Life in a Jar*. Who wrote the play and how was it inspired? What was the purpose of the play? Where has it been performed?

# Wordscramble

Here is a list of scrambled words that relate to the profile you read about Irena Sendler. Unscramble the letters and write the words correctly.

1. alndPo _____

2. strGWaowhtea _____

3. oetgZa _____

4. osnPiPwraiak _____

5. ebbir _____

6. lneIerdSaenr _____

7. orclsriwkoea _____

8. oltuaocHs _____

9. assKna _____

10. ooueascurg _____

# True or False

Create five true or false statements about this story. Present them to your family members. Mix up the true and false statements to keep everyone thinking. Be sure sure to make up an answer key so that your readers will know when they are correct. To see a sample True or False, turn to page 203.

## Using Context

Read the sentence and then look at the word in *italics*. Tell what you think that word means. Then look it up in a dictionary to confirm, or make sure of, the meaning. Tell someone about each word that you got correct. Remember, you will get better at understanding word meanings as you practice using context, or the words around a word.

1. Although she was saving their lives, it still must have felt like she was tearing children away from their parents. Irena did her best to *console* the families. (paragraph 5)

   I think *console* means: _____

   Dictionary definition: _____

   My meaning was: (Circle one)        correct        had correct parts        not close

2. Following her time in the *notorious* Pawaik Prison, Sendler carried on the work that had cost her so much, only now it was under a different name. (paragraph 9)

   I think *notorious* means: _____

   Dictionary definition: _____

   My meaning was: (Circle one)        correct        had correct parts        not close

3. In later years, Irena watched as the world began to forget about the horrors of the *Holocaust*. (paragraph 10)

   I think *Holocaust* means: _____

   Dictionary definition: _____

   My meaning was: (Circle one)        correct        had correct parts        not close

# Irena Sendler Word Search

```
F Z F C B G X F U R R L N Y I S U N B
I C N B G A T A H G M F P G N Q O R D
W S G B T M E Q Q P W P F O F T M E I
Y U H O D F A P K S N S S S T P A L P
V O G Q J C K J O U E I D E S G J D V
Z E U T L P F L U L R U H A F Z K N E
Z G J K S M W W C P A G S G S P W E G
F A A Y I U J G K K W N B E G C Z S K
M R S R Q I A I F A A U D Q E E S A E
I U R O G J A C S K I F B C N B O N L
R O Z W G W P R O A T S C Z K I B E L
M C A K A V A F W L P D E J M R V R U
X V F P J W A N J X O Z I H F B H I D
I K C G Y O U Q M N I H Y O Z L M J G
C H R J G F R E K R O W L A I C O S Q
```

## Word Bank

| | |
|---|---|
| bribe | Pawaik Prison |
| courageous | Poland |
| Holocaust | social worker |
| Irena Sendler | Warsaw Ghetto |
| Kansas | Zegota |

# *Irena Sendler Crossword*

**Across**

2. the first country to be invaded by Germany at the start of World War II

4. paying someone in order for them to do something you want

5. name of the Polish underground organization Irena worked with

6. place where Irena was held by the Nazis

9. name of the sixteen block area the Jews were forced into in Poland

10. Irena's profession

**Down**

1. to be extremely brave

3. woman who saved 2,500 Jewish children during the Holocaust

7. American state where four high schoolers wrote a play about Irena's life

8. the systematic efforts to destroy the Jewish people by Nazi Germany

# Winston Churchill

It was during an annual ball held by his parents that a strong-willed and impatient Winston Churchill decided to make his appearance. Never mind that he was two months early, or that guests from around England were present, Winston Leonard Spencer Churchill had made his own plan. He was born during the very early morning hours of November 30th, 1874.

Winston Churchill is remembered as the Lion of Britain. Without him, many have wondered whether the Allied forces would have been able to win the battle for Europe during World War II. Churchill's charismatic determination as Prime Minister of England gave courage to his entire nation. They endured Germany's threats and attacks like no other. In one of his most famous speeches, Churchill shows us the strength of his character:

> *"...never give in, never give in, never, never, never, never—in nothing, great or small, large or petty—never give in except to convictions of honour and good sense. Never yield to force; never yield to the apparently overwhelming might of the enemy."*

Winston Churchill had a very different childhood than what you might have come to expect from the small town heroes you learn about. The Churchills were cold toward their young son. They found more time for their various social pursuits than for Winston. He was forced to find comfort in the attention of his nanny. She instilled in him the faith and principles that would seize his heart.

As a young boy, Winston was sent away to several distinguished schools of his time. He managed to struggle through most of them. The determination that he would later be known for was undoubtedly shaped during these years. He had to fight for most everything. Though bright, Winston had to work very hard to succeed. He was also a bit scrawny as a child and had to push himself to meet the athletic abilities of those around him. He was prone to illness, and struggled with a slight speech impediment. But these difficulties would only make Winston stronger. In 1882, he was accepted into the British version of West Point, a military academy named Sandhurst. It was only after taking the entrance examination three times that he earned his acceptance. Once there, Churchill studied things that were actually of interest to him and he excelled because of it, graduating eigth out of a class of 150.

Following Sandhurst, Winston set out to make a name for himself. He always felt the call of destiny on his life—it pushed and guided him. He would seek out chances to prove his courage, putting himself in the midst of any military undertakings he could. Winston also discovered that he could quicken his fame by writing about his exploits. Soon he had published his first book, *The Story of the Malakind Field Force*. It became quite popular. A turning point in Winston's life occurred when he was selected to go to South Africa as a War Correspondent for the Morning Post. The Boer War, which lasted from 1899-1902, was a war between the British Empire and the Boer republics of South Africa.

Though Churchill fought fiercely, and made some heroic efforts, he was captured along with the group that he traveled with and taken to a Boer prison camp. A determined Churchill could not be held captive for long however, and escaped after only weeks of imprisonment. What was even more miraculous than his escape, though, was what happened next. After finding a train station, Winston waited for the opportune moment to stow away. Once on a train, he was carried to an unknown destination where he hopped off before daybreak. Thinking that another opportunity to stow away would come, he waited by the train tracks. But none came. Now desperate, he walked along the tracks looking for another option. Nearly ready to collapse, Winston decided that he had no choice but to ask for the help of a farmer. Of all the houses he could have come across within a 20-mile radius, Winston Churchill later found out that he knocked on the only door that would not lead to his return to the Boer prison camp. His remarkable story caught the attention of the press, and soon the world would hear of it too. In his own words:

*"I realized with awful force that no exercise of my own feeble wit and strength could save me from my enemies, and without the assistance of that High Power which interferes with the eternal sequence of causes and effects more often than we are always prone to admit, I could never succeed. I prayed long and earnestly for help and guidance. My prayer, as it seems to me, was swiftly and wonderfully answered."*

Upon his return to England, Winston Churchill focused his attention on politics. He was elected to the House of Commons in 1900. It was a position that he would hold off and on for the rest of his life. From there he moved up the ladder, becoming President of the Board of Trade, Home Secretary, and finally First Lord of the Admiralty in the years leading up to World War I. Winston Churchill was one of the first to see the need in strengthening Britain's military. Before the onset of World War I, Churchill helped modernize the navy and set up the Royal Naval Air Service.

During these years, Winston also took the vow of marriage to a woman named Clementine Hozier. The two shared a deep love for one another over the more than fifty-five years that they were married. During unstable times, Churchill found solace within his family. When he became a father in 1909, it was a joyous day in the Churchill household. He promised to never be like his own cold and distant parents, and he wasn't. Winston lavished affection on his children. The war hero and statesman showed the world that he also had a more gentle side.

World War I taught Winston Churchill some important lessons that he would not soon forget. One incident nearly ended his political career. The Dardanelles campaign began as a brilliant tactical plan. It was created to lighten the level of resistance against Allied forces in France. Churchill backed this plan as he saw a need for the new strategy. Problems first arose when the number of men needed to complete the mission swiftly was denied. This was followed by delays and costly hesitation. The plan wasn't the problem, but the way British commanders executed it caused a catastrophic defeat. Nevertheless, Churchill became the point for blame. He lost his position as the Fist Lord of the Admiralty, and was forced into a time of isolation and depression. During these wilderness years, Winston published several books and slowly worked to overcome the incident.

It wasn't until the gathering tension of World War II that Winston Churchill was again seen as a hero in his nation. Churchill warned of an impending second war with Germany long before others would take notice of it. In 1933, he tried to sound the alarm, but none would listen. One of the greatest gifts Churchill possessed was the way he could assess a situation accurately and honestly. Unafraid of the truth, he could foresee conflict and prepare accordingly. It was because of Winston's insight that once England realized he had been right all along, he was reinstated as the First Lord of the Admiralty. By 1940, England was getting tired of her current Prime Minister, who had let Germany grow strong. The time had come for Winston Churchill's most important hour. The King sent for the sixty-six year old Winston. He sent for a man who had watched a war develop with Germany once before, one who had shown the depths of his courage during his own years as a soldier, and one who had even predicted their current situation. Winston Churchill was asked to take the position of Prime Minister.

So Winston came forward to be the leader that his nation needed, that the world would need. In his first speech to the House of Commons the new Prime Minister made his stance clear:

> *"We have before us an ordeal of the most grievous kind. We have before us many, many long months of struggle and of suffering. You ask, what is our policy? I can say: It is to wage war, by sea, land, and air, with all our might and with all the strength that God can give us; to wage war against a monstrous tyranny, never surpassed in the dark, lamentable catalogue of human crime. That is our policy. You ask, what is our aim? I can answer in one word: It is victory, victory at all costs, victory in spite of all terror, victory, however long and hard the road may be."*

When the people of England needed courage, Winston Churchill spoke words of encouragement. When they were hopeless, he instilled hope. When they needed a leader who was not afraid to show that he cared, Churchill wept before them. The confidence Winston had in the strength of his people and in the cause of liberty was contagious. But he did not just inspire them with his words, he invoked their courage with his actions. Sleeping in a bunker, stepping onto the battlefields, he put himself in the middle of his country's suffering.

Winston wrote of his role in his book, *The Second World War*. He said, "I felt as if I were walking with destiny, and that all my past life had been but a preparation for this hour and this trial." He understood the importance of the battle, giving over all of his efforts to it. Because of the disaster at the Dardanelles, he stayed closely connected to all military plans, serving his country with a seemingly endless energy. In another famous speech, Winston called to his people to preserve the faith, and to remember that their actions went much farther than the present:

> *"Hitler knows that he will have to break us in this Island or lose the war. If we can stand up to him, all Europe may be free and the life of the world may move forward into broad, sunlit uplands. But if we fail, then the whole world, including the United States, including all that we have known and cared for, will sink into the abyss of a new Dark Age made more sinister, and perhaps more protracted, by the lights of perverted science. Let us therefore brace ourselves to our duties, and so bear ourselves that, if the British Empire and its Commonwealth last for a thousand years, men will still say, 'This was their finest hour.' "*

As you know, Hitler was defeated, and it was a victory felt around the world. Because of his incredible influence, Winston Churchill has been called one of the greatest leaders of the 20th century. Earning the respect of many nations, Winston was honored by his Queen with Knighthood, awarded the French Cross of Liberation, the American Freedom Award, and became an honorary citizen of the United States.

On the morning of January 25th, 1965, at ninety years of age, Winston Churchill retired from the struggles of this world. We are forever indebted to this man for what he did, and for the courage in which he stood.

## Discussion

One of the most powerful men in history, Adolf Hitler, was afraid of Winston Churchill. Why do you think that someone so influential would be afraid of him? Winston Churchill has been called one of the greatest leaders of the 20th century. In your opinion, what was it that made him such an exceptional leader?

NORTH SEA

IRELAND

UNITED KINGDOM

London

CELTIC SEA

ENGLISH CHANNEL

FRANCE

# Timeline Activity

Put things in perspective. Place Winston Churchill's figure on the timeline in the year 1940, which was when he became Prime Minister of England. Then identify two other events that happened in history during his life and add them to your timeline. You might also add a symbol or picture that represents this event.

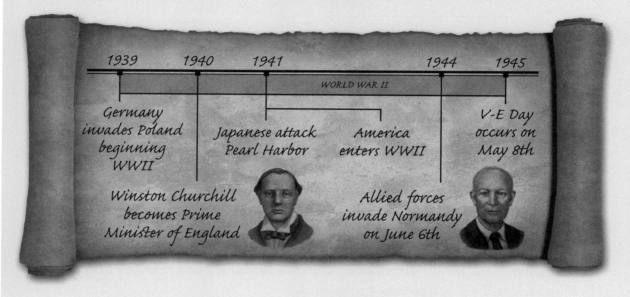

1939   1940   1941   1944   1945

WORLD WAR II

Germany invades Poland beginning WWII

Japanese attack Pearl Harbor

America enters WWII

V-E Day occurs on May 8th

Winston Churchill becomes Prime Minister of England

Allied forces invade Normandy on June 6th

# Activity

Winston Churchill is known for his oratory expertise. He is remembered for the way his speeches were delivered, as well as the eloquent words he spoke. Choose your favorite speech given by Winston Churchill and take on his character as you read it aloud to your family members.

## Wordscramble

Here is a list of scrambled words that relate to the profile you read about Winston Churchill. Unscramble the letters and write the words correctly.

1. orBareW  _____
2. nhSasdrtu  _____
3. etmneHreolzCinei  _____
4. alrorWIWdI  _____
5. oAledlrtHfi  _____
6. alnEgnd  _____
7. ePsmnrirMiite  _____
8. nosuComfHemsoo  _____
9. rlihoncWstuilhnC  _____
10. artroo  _____

## True or False

Create five true or false statements about this story. Present them to your family members. Mix up the true and false statements to keep everyone thinking. Be sure sure to make up an answer key so that your readers will know when they are correct. To see a sample True or False, turn to page 203.

## Write a Letter

If you could speak to Winston Churchill, what would you say? Would you tell him how grateful you are for his sacrifices? Or maybe you would ask him questions about what it was like to do what he did. Write a letter or an email to Winston Churchill. You can also make a postcard instead of writing a letter or email. On your postcard, create a scene that represents the person you read about. Include at least one quote that you think represents this person well.

# Winston Churchill Word Search

```
R T M P E X O U D H P D E U J E H X Z
Q A S R G Y F O X O R A T O R Z O K P
N D W R B Y S L E B I B N S H H U L L
G O O R U J W V Z J M L E H V R S Q K
N L R D E H F N P C E S Z I N I E J O
O F L J N O D N J N M W X F O I O F K
G H D V G L B N C Z I V I C P L F Z T
R I W V L Y T D A E N I I E X I C I B
A T A K A X Y G D S I D V P Z M O Y B
P L R O N D L I B J S W L K K U M E C
E E I A D F F C Z T T A D H V X M F A
D R I L P P L I S U E Z J U R H O E E
W I N S T O N C H U R C H I L L N Y B
T C Y A I W X U N N Y H R H P O S X K
S T R E I Z O H E N I T N E M E L C J
```

## Word Bank

Adolf Hitler

Boer War

Clementine Hozier

England

House of Commons

orator

Prime Minister

Sandhurst

Winston Churchill

World War II

# Winston Churchill Crossword

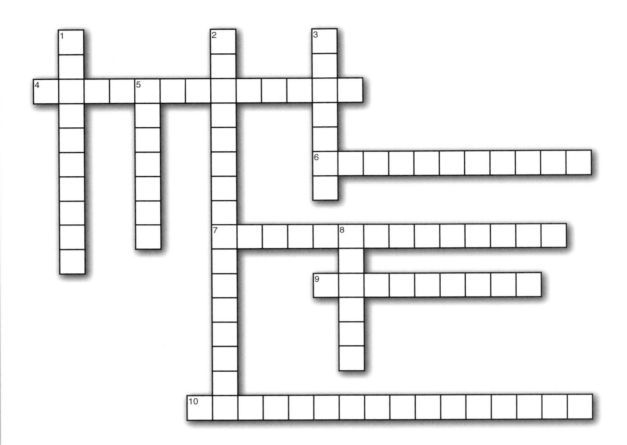

## Across

4. the elected leader of government in Great Britain
6. ruler of Nazi Germany
7. Parliament in the United Kingdom
9. British version of the military academy at West Point
10. the wife of Winston Churchill

## Down

1. war between 1939-1945
2. Prime Minister of England during World War II
3. a war between the British Empire and the Boer republics of South Africa
5. country of Great Britain
8. someone who is skilled in public speaking

# Dr. Charles Drew

A significant hero in World War II lived and died without great recognition. His name was Dr. Charles Drew. He was a medical pioneer who saved thousands of lives during the war.

How was it that a doctor saved so many? It was through the preservation of blood. Up until Dr. Drew discovered a process that could keep blood viable, there was no way to preserve it for more than several days at a time. The need for blood was never as high as it was during World War II, which is why Dr. Drew worked so hard to make this scientific discovery and why it was so heroic.

Charles Drew was born in Washington D.C. on June 3, 1904. He was the oldest of five children. Drew's father laid carpet for a living and his mother was a teacher. Throughout his life, Charles required excellence of himself. He was raised to be hard working, diligent, and well-mannered. These were qualities that he carried on throughout his life. When he was twelve years old, tragedy struck the family. Drew's sister died of tuberculosis. This was one of the reasons that he later became interested in a medical profession.

A dedicated student and a talented athlete during his high school years, Drew won the award for all-around best athlete. This led him to receive a scholarship to Amherst College, in Massachusetts. There, he was again awarded for his outstanding athletic ability. Following Amherst, Drew taught at a college for a couple of years saving up money for what would be his true calling, medicine. He went on to attend medical school at McGill University in Montreal, Canada. While there, he began to research blood transfusions. Drew also became a member of the Medical Honorary Society and graduated from McGill second in his class, with Master of Surgery and Doctor of Medicine degrees. In the year 1935, he returned to the United States.

After receiving a fellowship at Columbia University in New York City, he continued his study of blood preservation. In 1940, he completed a thesis on Banked Blood which was compiled from exhaustive research. With this thesis, Drew became the first African-American to receive a medical science degree from Columbia University. It was while there that he made his most important discoveries. Blood is primarily made up of plasma (about 55%), which is a yellowish substance composed mostly of water, proteins, and salts. The other large part (about 45%) is red blood cells. Dr. Drew developed a method of separating the red blood cells from the plasma and storing them separately. With this technique, he could reconstruct the two at a later time, when needed. A monumental breakthrough, this allowed blood to be stored away and saved over a greater period of time. He also showed that although different blood types can only receive whole blood from the same type, blood plasma can be given to anyone. This was great news for those in emergency situations. Someone with an immediate need for blood could be given plasma as a substitute until there was an opportunity for proper treatment.

It was the looming war in Europe that spurred on Dr. Drew's work. He knew that many lives could be saved on and off the battlefields with his help. In an urgent medical situation one of the most vital tools a doctor can have at his disposal is blood. Without enough, a person has no chance for survival. There is also no substitute for blood. It cannot be manufactured; therefore the only way for blood to be stored is through volunteers who are willing to give it. So Dr. Drew organized the first blood bank drive, Blood for Britain, which was a program that collected blood to aid England as they were battling Germany. As director of this successful campaign, Dr. Drew stored an enormous amount of blood plasma that would save many lives.

As it became evident that war in Europe would soon involve the United States, the government enlisted the American Red Cross to begin gathering a stockpile of blood reserves. Dr. Drew, as the leading authority on the subject, headed up the project for the Red Cross. He established our country's largest blood banking system, and worked tirelessly to aid the war effort. Sadly though, he lived during a time of racial segregation. When the military sent out an initiative to separate the blood of African American donors from that of whites, Dr. Drew resigned.

He then returned to Washington D.C. to work and teach at Howard University and the accompanying Freedmen's Hospital. There, Drew became professor of surgery and chief surgeon. In 1944, he received the celebrated Spingarn Medal from the NAACP (National Association for the Advancement of Colored People) for his outstanding contribution to humankind.

Tragically, on April 1st, 1950, Dr. Charles Drew died from injuries suffered during an automobile accident. He was on his way to a medical conference, and only 45 years old at the time. Remembered as the father of the blood bank, Dr. Drew's impact was enormous and extremely timely. Someone is in need of blood every two seconds. Stored blood is used for surgeries, cancer patients, trauma victims, and in a case of war, the need is great. Just one pint of donated blood can save as many as three lives. Without Dr. Drew's research, countless lives would have been lost. His future was still so bright when he was stolen by a car accident. He was a beloved husband, father to four children, and a teacher who fully dedicated himself to raising up generations of excellent young surgeons. Undoubtedly, he would have done much more if given the chance, but thankfully, he left us with revolutionary knowledge and medical gains.

## Discussion

Why was Dr. Drew's discovery so important? Why do you think he is not very well known today? Would you consider him to be a hero of World War II?

Find someone you know who has given blood before. Talk with them about why they chose to do it, and what it was like. Would you give blood? Talk with your teacher about why, or why not.

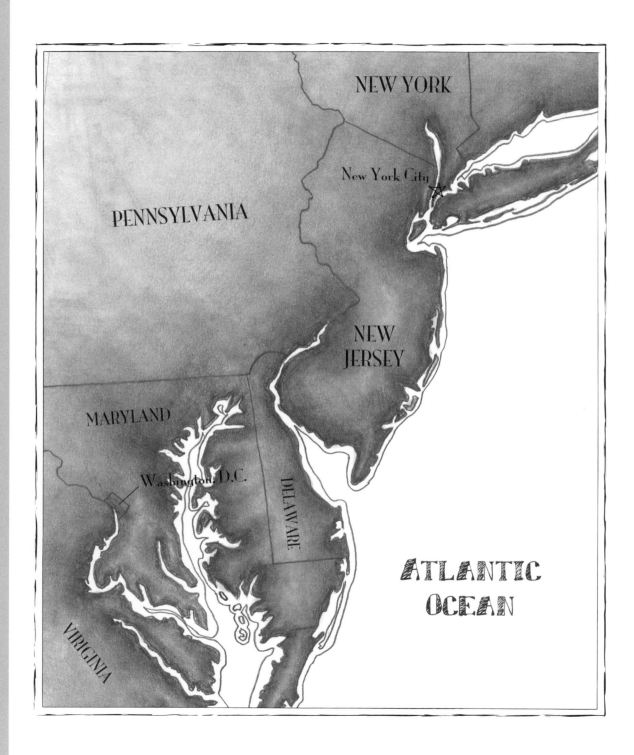

# Timeline Activity

Put things in perspective. Place Dr. Charles Drew's figure on the timeline in the year 1940, which was when he completed his thesis on "Banked Blood." Then identify two other events that happened in history during his life and add them to your timeline. You might also add a symbol or picture that represents this event.

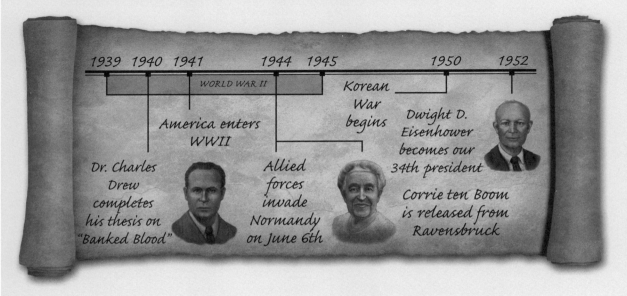

# Activity

Talk with your parent about the medical supplies in your home. Do you have a first aid kit? With your parents' permission, learn about basic first aid supplies in your home, and how you would use them. Does your family have a plan in case of an emergency? Do you think it is a good idea to have a first aid kit in your home, along with an emergency plan?

# Wordscramble

Here is a list of scrambled words that relate to the profile you read about Dr. Charles Drew. Unscramble the letters and write the words correctly.

1. teleaht _____

2. taovienpesrr _____

3. ChgsWDionnat _____

4. dCorsRes _____

5. amapls _____

6. rwDeelrDaCshr _____

7. funssitaorn _____

8. ootcdr _____

9. syUtibrlneivomauiC _____

10. nlbkooadb _____

# True or False

Create five true or false statements about this story. Present them to your family members. Mix up the true and false statements to keep everyone thinking. Be sure sure to make up an answer key so that your readers will know when they are correct. To see a sample True or False, turn to page 203.

# *Using Context*

Read the sentence and then look at the word in *italics*. Tell what you think that word means. Then look it up in a dictionary to confirm, or make sure of, the meaning. Tell someone about each word that you got correct. Remember, you will get better at understanding word meanings as you practice using context, or the words around a word.

1. Up until Dr. Drew discovered a process that could keep blood *viable*, there was no way to preserve it for more than several days at a time. (paragraph 2)

   I think *viable* means: _____

   Dictionary definition: _____

   My meaning was: (Circle one)     correct     had correct parts     not close

2. He also showed that although different blood types can only receive whole blood from the same type, *blood plasma* can be given to anyone. (paragraph 5)

   I think *blood plasma* means: _____

   Dictionary definition: _____

   My meaning was: (Circle one)     correct     had correct parts     not close

3. There is also no substitute for blood. It cannot be *manufactured*; therefore the only way for blood to be stored is through volunteers who are willing to give it. (paragraph 6)

   I think *manufactured* means: _____

   Dictionary definition: _____

   My meaning was: (Circle one)     correct     had correct parts     not close

# Dr. Charles Drew Word Search

```
D L L W V W J A C X J Z M R V F K M B
Y T I S R E V I N U A I B M U L O C C
K D R C H A R L E S D R E W U J V H S
Z Z O Q T D A U X A I Q B W L K O J S
N L G F P R E S E R V A T I O N G N O
P I L A Z H A Z T L B A P K Q K H A R
C C D N O T G N I H S A W X N V F X C
U P O P Q E H T S W Z J Z A W E O Q D
L P C G F U Q V L F Z L B M D X M A E
S L T S Q H E S Q B U D G O S I I B R
Z N O L W K M O S R O S C S G B K G S
G G R Z L I R N Z O I J I Y D M E O M
H F Q U I N S P L A S M A O N N X I N
N M I B T Q N B P O A G K B N T E C C
C H E T E L H T A X E Q A O J F C A F
```

## Word Bank

athlete

blood bank

Charles Drew

Columbia University

doctor

plasma

preservation

Red Cross

transfusion

Washington D.C.

# Dr. Charles Drew Crossword

## Across

3. medical pioneer in blood preservation
6. the action of being kept safe
7. a person who plays sports
9. prestigious university located in New York City
10. the act of transferring blood into a person's body

## Down

1. a yellowish substance made up of mostly water proteins and salts
2. a place where blood is stored
4. organization that provides relief during disasters
5. America's capitol
8. a person who engages in the medical profession

# Dwight D. Eisenhower

**D**wight D. Eisenhower, or Ike as his friends called him, was a fiery and stubborn young man. He had inherited his father's temper, but with this disposition also came a fierce determination that would serve him well in the years to come. Ike was raised in the small town of Abilene, Kansas. The third of seven boys, his family was well respected in the community. They were church-going people with strict standards that pushed Ike to become a hardworking man.

In 1911, Ike's future was shaped by his appointment to the U.S. Military Academy at West Point in upstate New York. West Point is the foremost military academy in the country, graduating presidents, celebrated generals, and over seventy cadets who went on to receive the highest military decoration, the Medal of Honor. Eisenhower couldn't just enroll at West Point. He had to score well on an entrance exam and receive a recommendation from a Kansas state senator. Since his family did not have the money to send him to college, and a West Point education is paid for by the Army, Ike decided to take the entrance examinations.

West Point's motto, "Duty, Honor, Country," would stay with Eisenhower the rest of his life. He graduated in 1915 and was stationed in San Antonio, Texas. Soon after his arrival in Texas, Ike met a young woman by the name of Mamie Doud. The two were instantly attracted to each other and married July 1st of 1916. The following year, the United States entered World War I. Despite his efforts to be sent overseas, the young Eisenhower did not see combat in the First World War. Instead, he received the promotion of Captain and was sent to Georgia to train officer candidates.

At that time, tanks were the newest weapons in warfare. Therefore, soldiers needed to be trained in using them. Eisenhower was assigned to this task at Camp Meade, Maryland. While there, he met George Patton. Their friendship would prove very important during the latter years of World War II. When Eisenhower left Camp Meade he had received a promotion to major, and an assignment in Pennsylvania to lead the army's first tank corps.

Upon recommendation, Eisenhower was accepted into the army's Command and General Staff School at Fort Leavenworth, Kansas. Here, he studied war strategies, combat situations, and battle planning. Ike graduated at the top of his class of nearly 300. He also attended the Army War College, graduating first in his class again. Eisenhower, gaining notoriety, then worked under such famous men as Generals John J. Pershing and Douglas McArthur.

In 1939, Germany invaded Poland. The Nazi leader of Germany, Hitler, had made his move. For years, the Axis Coalition (Germany, Italy and Japan) had been building up their militaries, preparing for the day they planned to take over the countries around them. World War II, the most widespread war in history, had begun. The Allied Coalition mainly consisted of Great Britain, the Soviet Union (Russia), and the United States. They were known as the "Big Three." Essentially, there were two wars going on, one in Europe and one in the Pacific. The Allied forces decided that their biggest threat was Germany and the war in Europe, so they devoted most of their resources there. On June 11th, 1942, Eisenhower was chosen as the Commander of the European Theater of Operations and was sent to England.

Eisenhower's first campaign was called Operation Torch. It was a plan to take back Nazi-controlled North Africa. If successful, the Allies would have control over the majority of the Mediterranean Sea. In November of 1942, Operation Torch began. British and U.S. troops landed in Algeria and Morocco. By early May, the German forces were driven out, but not without sacrifice. There were many casualties, and Eisenhower's skill was questioned more than once. It was a learning experience for both the U.S. troops and Eisenhower.

Operation Overlord was the code name for what would be the largest amphibious invasion in history. With Eisenhower in charge as the Supreme Allied Commander, it was a mission to invade Normandy, France, in the hopes of taking back Western

Europe. Conditions would have to be just right. The troops needed warm enough weather for the anticipated months of fighting. They would need clear skies for the aerial attack, and the tides had to be at the right depth for the landing craft to carry soldiers to shore. It took all of Eisenhower's years in training and knowledge of military history to devise this master plan. Winston Churchill called it, *"the most difficult and complicated operation that has ever taken place."*

In the hours before Operation Overlord, Eisenhower could be found among the men of the 101st Airborne. As they prepared for deployment, Ike knew that he couldn't offer them much comfort. But he could shake their hands and thank them for their service. He could help calm their nerves by making small talk, and remind them of how proud their country was of them. The invasion began with a 12,000 plane airborne attack, then 150,000 troops were carried to the beaches of Normandy on the morning of June 6th. By nightfall, the Allied forces had gained a foothold in Nazi controlled France. D-Day, as it is known, was a success that marked the beginning of the end of the war. By September, the Allies had liberated France. Eisenhower became a five star general, the highest rank in the U.S. Army. In his own words:

> *"War is a grim, cruel business, a business justified only as a means of sustaining the forces of good against those of evil."*

World War II was a necessary but grim business. It was because of men like Dwight Eisenhower that the forces of good prevailed. When the Germans surrendered on May 7th, 1945, Eisenhower sent a message to the U.S. Chief of Staff, George Marshall, communicating the victory. Part of the message he received in return read, *"You have made history, great history for the good of mankind and you have stood for all we hope for and admire in an officer of the United States Army."*

Following the war, Eisenhower became the president of Columbia University. A couple of years later, he was asked to command the forces of the newly formed NATO (North Atlantic Treaty Organization). And in 1953, Eisenhower continued his career of serving America, though this time in a very different way. With the campaign slogan "I like Ike," Eisenhower became the 34th President of the United States by an overwhelming majority. True to his roots, he never pretended to be anything other than a man from a small town trying to steer his country in the right direction. Eisenhower, unlike the many men who run for office in order to gain power, was a reluctant candidate. He only ran because he felt his country needed him and he couldn't say no. Four years later, America voted for another Eisenhower term. Proving to be the right man at a crucial time in our nation's history, Ike guided the country during the early years of such events as the Cold War, the Vietnam Conflict, and the Space Race. He enforced the desegregation of schools in Washington D.C., and supported the the Civil Rights Movement by signing the Civil Rights Acts of 1957 and 1960 into law. On Flag Day in 1954, Eisenhower signed a bill that added the words "under God" to the Pledge of Allegiance. Also during the Eisenhower years, Hawaii and Alaska became the 49th and 50th states.

He was still as popular and trusted at the end of his presidency as he was at the beginning. Some say that if Eisenhower were able to run for a third term in office, he would have won again. Below is an excerpt from his farewell address. It is the final prayer of a President for the future of his country, and of a man who devoted his life to his nation:

> *"We pray that peoples of all faiths, all races, all nations, may have their great human needs satisfied; that those now denied opportunity shall come to enjoy it to the full; that all who yearn for freedom may experience its spiritual blessings; that those who have freedom will understand, also, its heavy responsibilities; that all who are insensitive to the needs of others will learn charity; that the scourges of poverty, disease and ignorance will be made to disappear from the earth, and that, in the goodness of time, all peoples will come to live together in a peace guaranteed by the binding force of mutual respect and love."*

## Discussion

Try to find a friend or family member who was an adult during World War II, or is related to someone who was. If you cannot find a World War II era person, then interview a veteran of any war to find out where they served, what their feeling was about their experiences, and how it changed them.

GREAT BRITAIN

ENGLISH CHANNEL

Utah

Omaha

Gold

Juno

Sword

FRANCE

ATLANTIC OCEAN

## Timeline Activity

Put things in perspective. Place Dwight D. Eisenhower's figure on the timeline in the year 1944, which was when the invasion of Normandy by the Allied forces began. Then identify two other events that happened in history during his life and add them to your timeline. You might also add a symbol or picture that represents this event.

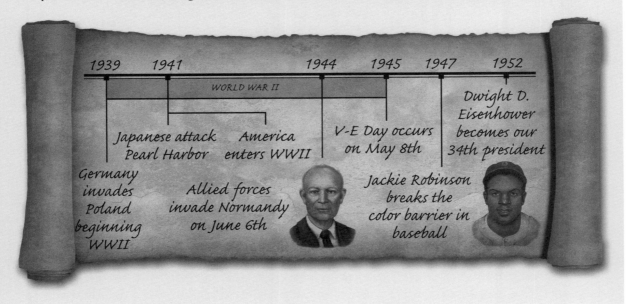

## Activity

Dwight D. Eisenhower led a life of service to our country. Is there a way that you or your parent could think of to support those who serve the country? One idea is to send thank you cards or care packages to your local servicemen.

## True or False

Create five true or false statements about this story. Present them to your family members. Mix up the true and false statements to keep everyone thinking. Be sure sure to make up an answer key so that your readers will know when they are correct. To see a sample True or False, turn to page 203.

## Write an Obituary

Write an obituary or a brief article that would appear about this person upon their passing. Since space is limited in a newspaper you may only use forty to forty-five words to describe this person. With such limited space, focus on the main events in their life. To see a sample obituary, turn to page 203.

# Dwight D. Eisenhower Word Search

```
A N Z M B V F U X N Z M R F P N O M U
D R O L R E V O N O I T A R E P O I K
G B R T J P M G A D T X I B E B Z Z R
F W A I F G N P J Y N N U F R O Y K H
P O P S P W K Q F Z V V S R H X A M E
G R S T A B A S D A S X Y G T I X O J
I L C O K U E G S V B C G H G G I Q M
Z D Q P M A M I E D O U D L I G S W H
L W E S T P O I N T W T T Z B J R B Q
H A V J Y N I F D X T W M T Y W M N E
R R E W O H N E S I E D T H G I W D J
H I Y L O R T C U K S J U I X W A K L
K I L J C E C B G D F D A E A D K U T
Q E O F I V E S T A R G E N E R A L L
B E U X Y M R A D E I L L A R T U Z Y
```

## Word Bank

Allied Army

Axis

Big Three

Dwight D. Eisenhower

five star general

invasion

Mamie Doud

Operation Overlord

West Point

World War II

# Dwight D. Eisenhower Crossword

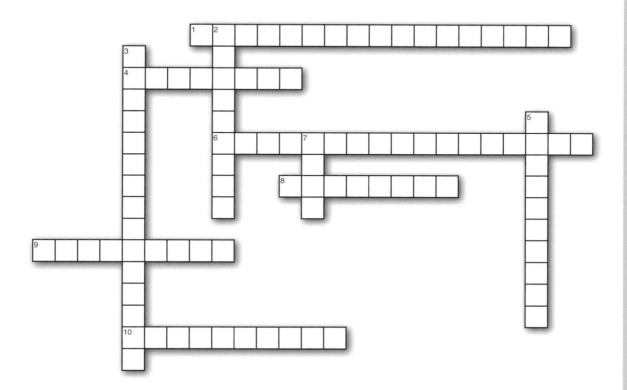

## Across

1. Supreme Allied Commander
4. the attack of a region or country in order to take it over
6. code name for the invasion of Normandy
8. coalition of Great Britain, the Soviet Union, and the United States
9. Dwight Eisenhower's wife
10. army of countries fighting against the Axis

## Down

2. foremost military academy in the country
3. highest rank in the U.S. Army
5. the most widespread war in history
7. coalition of Germany, Italy, and Japan

# Corrie ten Boom

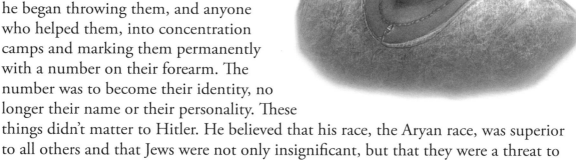

The most sinister and grievous part of World War II was not the fighting that took place, but the unspeakable acts that occurred behind enemy lines, in concentration camps. The only word to describe Adolf Hitler and his Nazi regime is evil, in its purest form. Hitler used both his army and civilians to round up all of the Jews he could find in Europe. First, he forced them to wear a Jewish star on their clothes, signaling to others their "brand." Then, he began throwing them, and anyone who helped them, into concentration camps and marking them permanently with a number on their forearm. The number was to become their identity, no longer their name or their personality. These things didn't matter to Hitler. He believed that his race, the Aryan race, was superior to all others and that Jews were not only insignificant, but that they were a threat to the perfect world he envisioned.

This is the story of a woman who endured just such a concentration camp. History can teach us many things if we are only willing to learn. The story you're about to read has so many rich lessons to offer. Through it all, this woman possessed a rare and valuable gift. It was the undefeatable spirit of Corrie ten Boom that saved her.

Corrie was born in the Netherlands, on April 15th, 1892. Her father was a watchmaker, who worked in a shop attached to their house. It was a family business and Corrie became the first woman in Holland to be licensed as a watchmaker. The ten Booms were a very close family. Casper, or papa, was widely known for his craftsmanship and kindness. The entire town of Haarlem knew and loved the family. Corrie had three sisters and one brother. Sadly, her mother died after having a stroke when she was only sixty-three. A family of strong faith, Casper read the Bible aloud to his household every morning.

On May 10th, 1940, Germany invaded Corrie's homeland. Within six days they surrendered, and so began the Nazi occupation of Holland. The ten Boom family, seeing the growing wickedness around them, chose to do what they could to help, no matter the cost. Corrie, her father, and her sister Betsie opened up their home as an underground refuge. Jews who were trying to escape came to stay with the ten Booms and to gain assistance in getting out of the area. Since the family was so well loved in Haarlem, they were able to get extra ration cards to feed their guests. They smuggled supplies into their home and built a secret wall in the top corner room of the house, which just happened to be Corrie's room. It was farthest from the entrance, and therefore, if raided, it would allow the most time for cover up. It is now known as "the hiding place." This name was later used as the title of the famous book written by Corrie ten Boom about her life.

They would run drills to see how fast they could make the house ready for inspection. They made up signals, and had a well laid out plan in case of emergency. They even had to think about things like what to do if the Gestapo (German secret police) arrived in the middle of the night. The police might feel the warmth of the beds and know that more than just the three were living there. Those hiding would need to cover their tracks by flipping over mattresses so that the beds would appear unoccupied. They also installed a buzzer alarm to warn of any incoming German soldiers.

It was a time of constant vigilance. Many people were smuggled in and out of the ten Boom house. It was a place of safety, care, and encouragement for those who stayed there. Sadly though, this is only part of Corrie's story. On February 18th, 1944, the Gestapo bombarded the house. Corrie was in her bedroom with the flu when her door flew open, and the six guests currently staying with them hurried into the hiding place. Corrie, her sister, and her father were roughly interrogated, and taken to a prison in The Hague. Separated and imprisoned, we can only begin to imagine their anguish. Unfortunately, Corrie's father, Casper, fell ill and died shortly after their arrest. One day at the prison, Corrie received a letter from home, and under the stamp were the words, *"all the watches in your closet are safe."* To know the six guests concealed in the hiding place had remained undiscovered, gave Corrie great encouragement.

After a few lightless and lonely months, the sisters were taken to an internment camp in Holland. And later, they were moved to the concentration camp of Ravensbruck, in Germany. Though indescribably awful, the two were at least reunited. Through the agony, their faith endured. Corrie had managed to smuggle in a small Bible, and with it the sisters held Bible studies, extending hope to others. During the day they were made to work hard labor, given next to no food, and beaten for misbehavior—which could simply amount to not working fast enough. Still, amongst the torture, the filth, and the humiliation, they encouraged those around them. In December, Corrie's companion and ever-faithful friend and sister, died within the walls of Ravensbruck. Then after several days, Corrie was inexplicably released. It was later discovered that she had been set free because of a clerical error. Shortly after her release, all the women Corrie's age held in Ravensbruck were killed.

*"No pit is so deep that He is not deeper still."* These were the words that Corrie and her sister stood by during their time in one of the darkest places the world has ever known. Following her return to Holland and the end of the war, Corrie began traveling and telling her story. First, she traveled throughout Europe, then the world. She opened a refuge house for those who had survived concentration camps, as she had. It was a place to receive healing from the deep wounds of the enemy. She also wrote several books. Her most popular, *The Hiding Place*, was made into a movie in 1975.

On one speaking occasion in Munich, Corrie came across someone that she had never planned to see again. One of the guards from the Ravensbruck concentration camp was standing before her. She recognized him right away. How could she forget? But he did not seem to remember her. The memories that rushed back paralyzed Corrie. He mentioned to her that he had been a guard in the place she was held. Then, he asked for the seemingly impossible, her forgiveness. Corrie had a choice to make and a lesson to teach to the world. After much mental struggle, she lifted her hand to the one held out by this man, knowing that if she could make it that far, the grace she needed would come. And with that action the words followed, *"I forgive you, brother! With all my heart."* It was no easy thing. All of Corrie's recollection told her not to. But she knew, from what she believed in and what she herself preached, it was the right choice. She said of that moment, *"I had never known God's love so intensely as I did then."*

Instead of locking her story away where it couldn't cause her pain, Corrie chose to share it with anyone who would listen. In her eyes, even if just a handful of people were impacted by her life, it was well worth the effort. Her legacy is one of bravery, self-sacrifice, courage through unthinkable suffering, refusal to be defeated, and most powerfully, forgiveness. After living a full life, Corrie died on her ninety-first birthday, in the year 1983.

## Timeline Activity

Put things in perspective. Place Corrie ten Boom's figure on the timeline in the year 1944, which was when she was released from Ravensbruck. Then identify two other events that happened in history during his life and add them to your timeline. You might also add a symbol or picture that represents this event.

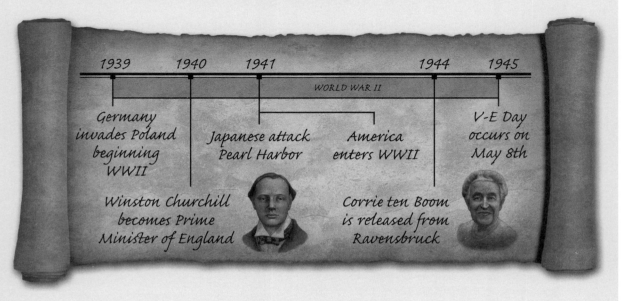

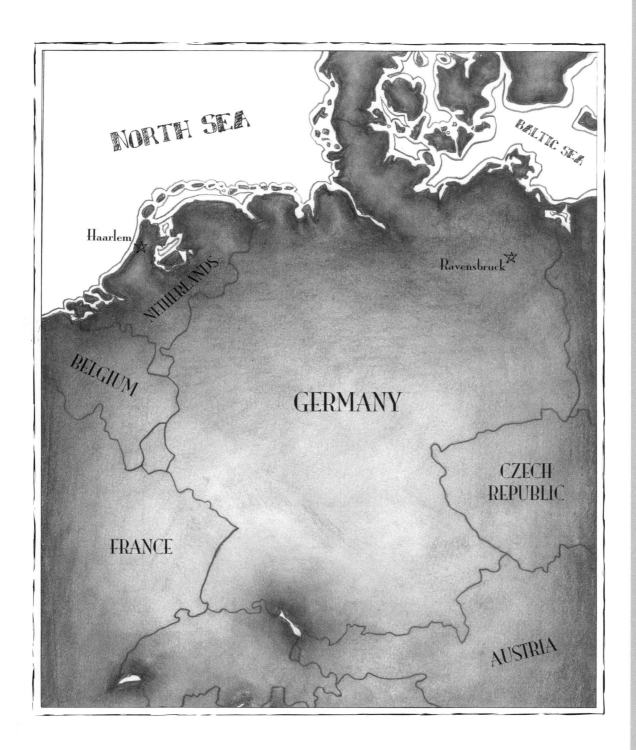

## Discussion

Corrie ten Boom's life gives many examples of the injustices done to her and her family. Yet she chose to take the path of forgiveness to those who persecuted her. Think of a time when someone treated you wrongly. Did you forgive them? If yes, was it difficult? Talk with your parent about the importance of forgiveness.

## Activity

Corrie and her sister Betsie used scripture to encourage each other during their most difficult times. Do you know anyone who is struggling with something difficult? With your parents' permission, make or buy a card to send to this person. Choose a verse or poem to include that you think might encourage them.

## Wordscramble

Here is a list of scrambled words that relate to the profile you read about Corrie ten Boom. Unscramble the letters and write the words correctly.

1. eieBts  _____

2. veRbcnauskr  _____

3. mekrhawtac  _____

4. chDut  _____

5. feisonvesrg  _____

6. tcconcimaponrntea  _____

7. eramlHa  _____

8. eoCrootneBrmi  _____

9. pacdgeinhil  _____

10. saptoeG  _____

## True or False

Create five true or false statements about this story. Present them to your family members. Mix up the true and false statements to keep everyone thinking. Be sure sure to make up an answer key so that your readers will know when they are correct. To see a sample True or False, turn to page 203.

## Using Context

Read the sentence and then look at the word in *italics*. Tell what you think that word means. Then look it up in a dictionary to confirm, or make sure of, the meaning. Tell someone about each word that you got correct. Remember, you will get better at understanding word meanings as you practice using context, or the words around a word.

1. The only word to describe Adolf Hitler and his Nazi *regime* is evil, in its purest form. (paragraph 1)

   I think *regime* means: _____

   Dictionary definition: _____

   My meaning was: (Circle one)      correct      had correct parts      not close

2. They *smuggled* supplies into their home and built a secret wall in the top corner room of the house, which just happened to be Corrie's room. (paragraph 4)

   I think *smuggled* means: _____

   Dictionary definition: _____

   My meaning was: (Circle one)      correct      had correct parts      not close

3. Then after several days, Corrie was *inexplicably* released. (paragraph 7)

   I think *inexplicably* means: _____

   Dictionary definition: _____

   My meaning was: (Circle one)      correct      had correct parts      not close

# Corrie ten Boom Word Search

```
C P M A C N O I T A R T N E C N O C N
G O M F H R A O H M N G V V J H T J P
H S T O N M Y R R M Z U Q C P A O W H
L L W R O M J I A K O D R N R X R G S
A H H G F B E T S I E M O T W X A I V
T Y H I D I N G P L A C E Z F F V R E
M X T V B D M E K C T I Y F Y Q E V M
Z R F E W Z U S T P R I M Z I K N C J
P D Q N G W R T V E I T U M A X S Z Y
C I E E V H W A C M I E S M A V B K E
F X B S T C Z P X H M R H U W P R T O
B W D S T R E O Z E W C R P B A U Y C
K O N U N A I W C N T P W O K D C M R
A Z U O P B Q H A A R L E M C X K Q E
Y M D M Y I H Y W N L O D T C U D R S
```

## Word Bank

Betsie

concentration camp

Corrie ten Boom

Dutch

forgiveness

Gestapo

Haarlem

hiding place

Ravensbruck

watchmaker

# Corrie ten Boom Crossword

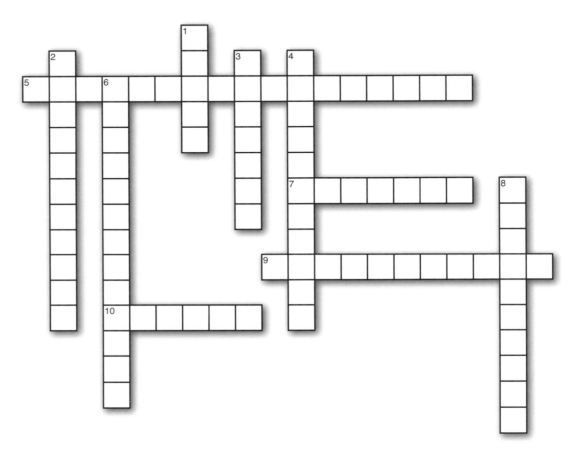

## Across

5. a place used by Nazis to hold Jews and those who helped them
7. German secret police
9. the concentration camp where Corrie and Betsie were held
10. Corrie's companion and ever faithful friend and sister

## Down

1. the predominant language spoken in Holland
2. the action of no longer holding someone's transgressions against them
3. Corrie's hometown
4. the secret room in the ten Boom home
6. concentration camp survivor author and motivational speaker
8. Casper ten Boom's profession

# Jackie Robinson

braham Lincoln and the Union Army won the battle of their time against slavery. Men and women all over the country cheered for their newfound freedom—it was a monumental victory! But it would be many years before African-Americans were treated as equals. Nearly a century would pass with hatred, segregation, and racial tension.

Jackie Robinson was not just a great baseball player, although he was certainly that. Jackie changed the game of baseball when he became the first African-American to play in the major leagues. But more important than that, through America's favorite pastime he helped change the country.

President of the Brooklyn Dodgers, Branch Rickey, had been looking for a very particular kind of player for a long time. He wanted a skillful player, and one whose character could withstand the challenge he had in mind. Branch Rickey knew that it was time for change. He also knew that it would not come without a fight. So he needed a well-calculated plan to ensure success. He needed a person who was willing to weather the persecution and the pressure. He needed Jackie Robinson.

Jackie was born in Cairo, Georgia, in the year 1919. After his father deserted them, Jackie's mother was left to raise five children on her own. She moved the family out to Pasadena, California, where her brother also lived. Mrs. Robinson worked as a maid and took odd jobs to provide for her family. Jackie greatly esteemed the selfless qualities his mother possessed. He undoubtedly learned his first lessons of character from her.

An athlete from the very beginning, Jackie loved sports. He was competitive in all he did, stating, *"Above anything else, I hate to lose."* At the Pasadena Junior College, Jackie participated in football, basketball, track, and baseball. He was a star athlete, and in 1938, he was named Most Valuable Player in baseball for the region. He continued his success at the University of California at Los Angeles, becoming the first student to letter in four sports.

Following his college years, Jackie became a member of the United States Army as the U.S. entered World War II. Within two years, he had been promoted to second lieutenant. But men who fought and died for the same country were still made to live separate lives based on color. One day during training, Jackie could not withstand the injustice any longer, and when asked to move to the back of a bus, he refused. This led to a court-martial, but all charges were eventually dropped and Jackie received an honorable discharge from the army.

Jackie got back into baseball in 1945. Playing for the Kansas City Monarchs in the Negro League, Jackie caught the attention of Branch Rickey. In August of that year, Rickey presented him with the now famously known opportunity. Rickey had one rule to go with his offer. He wanted Jackie to silence his critics with talent on the field, not attitude. During that first conversation Jackie had to ask, *"Mr. Rickey, are you looking for a Negro who is afraid to fight back?"* Rickey answered, *"Robinson, I'm looking for a ballplayer with guts enough not to fight back."*

Rickey knew that it was the only way to transformation. He told Robinson that once he proved himself on the field, things would be different. So Jackie took a leap toward equality, for which he faced unbridled hostility and persecution. It was not Jackie's personality to just sit by and watch injustice. He was a fighter. He always had been, and he always would be. So for every insult, for every player who threw a ball at his head, or slid toward him cleats first, he simply played harder and fought racism with sportsmanship. He never deceived himself into thinking that it would be easy. What kept him going was the knowledge that it was about so much more than just him. He believed that, *"A life is not important except in the impact it has on other lives."*

Jackie's journey began by playing for the Dodgers top farm team, the Montreal Royals. After a brilliant year, he was ready for the big leagues. The day that Jackie Robinson broke the color barrier of Major League Baseball was April 15th, 1947.

That first season started off a little slow for Jackie. But what no one could have imagined was that by the end of it, he would be named Rookie of the Year. It was the beginning of a stunning career, and soon Jackie started winning over his critics. Instead of being isolated by his teammates, they began standing by him. They saw how hard he worked, and the extent of his character. In one instance, second baseman Eddie Stanky, who knew of Robinson's pact with Rickey, called out to a merciless crowd saying, *"Why don't you yell at somebody who can answer back?"* Shortstop Pee Wee Reese showed his support by walking over to Jackie and putting his arm around him. This action spoke loud and clear. The Dodgers were ready to back up their teammate.

Jackie went on to lead the National League in stolen bases in 1947 and 1949. He was also the leading National League batter in 1949, and that year was named Most Valuable Player. The Brooklyn Dodgers won six pennants with Jackie's help, and in 1955, the World Series Championship against the seemingly unbeatable New York Yankees. The first year he was eligible, Jackie received the highest honor a baseball player can, and was elected into the Baseball Hall of Fame. Fittingly, in his last public appearance at the 1972 World Series, Jackie had the privilege of throwing the first ball. He died nine days later.

One young boy, who watched Jackie in amazement, ended up following his own dream of playing professional baseball. He is now known as one of the all-time greats, and up until recently Hank Aaron held the record for most career home runs. This baseball legend might not have had the opportunity if his hero, Jackie Robinson, hadn't had the courage to go first.

The moment that Jackie Robinson stepped onto that first major league field, he took a step that represented the beginning of change. The world watched with anticipation as he proved himself worthy of the challenge. That first step made the words of our forefathers ring truer and more loudly than ever before.

*"We hold these truths to be self-evident, that **all men** are created equal."*

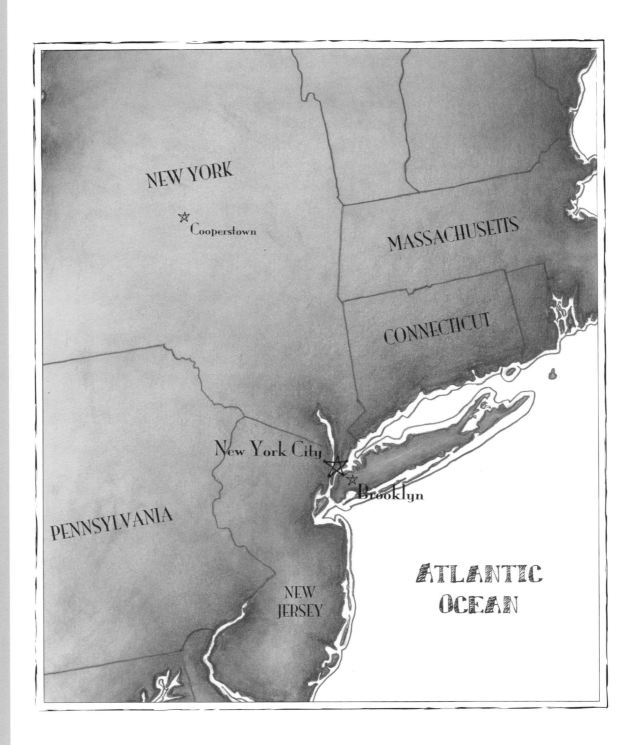

## Discussion

Have you ever been persecuted because you're different from others? If so, why? What about for something, or someone you stood up for? Do you agree with Jackie Robinson: *"A life is not important except in the impact it has on other lives"*? Why, or why not?

## Timeline Activity

Put things in perspective. Place Jackie Robinson's figure on the timeline in the year 1947, which was when he broke the color barrier in baseball. Then identify two other events that happened in history during his life and add them to your timeline. You might also add a symbol or picture that represents this event.

| 1945 | 1947 | 1952 | 1957 | 1960 |

Japan surrenders ending WWII

Jackie Robinson breaks the color barrier in baseball

Dwight D. Eisenhower becomes our 34th president

Space race begins with the launching of Sputnik

Civil Rights movement begins

## Activity

Learn more about Branch Rickey. What motivated him to find a player like Jackie? With your parent's permission, watch the movie about Jackie Robinson's life, starring Jackie Robinson, called *The Jackie Robinson Story*.

## True or False

Create five true or false statements about this story. Present them to your family members. Mix up the true and false statements to keep everyone thinking. Be sure sure to make up an answer key so that your readers will know when they are correct. To see a sample True or False, turn to page 203.

## Wordscramble

Here is a list of scrambled words that relate to the profile you read about Jackie Robinson. Unscramble the letters and write the words correctly.

1. taRnoyMollares _____

2. eskooRJacinbin _____

3. deaanPsa _____

4. pitimovtcee _____

5. lbsablea _____

6. oedgDsr _____

7. YoerkNw _____

8. elmafFoaHl _____

9. eacRhBirnkcy _____

10. nHankaorA _____

## Write a Letter

If you could speak to Jackie Robinson, what would you say? Would you tell him how grateful you are for his sacrifices? Or maybe you would ask him questions about what it was like to do what he did. Write a letter or an email to Jackie Robinson. You can also make a postcard instead of writing a letter or email. On your postcard, create a scene that represents the person you read about. Include at least one quote that you think represents this person well.

# Jackie Robinson Word Search

```
G Z S Q M G D F R Q H X S W B Q K I Y
D S L U Y X N D P P C K L K H H J J Y
V N A D O D G E R S I O B Y X Z A Q E
X C Y T A H L Q J Z D A A R X C I N K
O O O V E A V O E O W Z I N K J O R C
F M R R G L K R O Y W E N I G R R C I
A P L D U L P N B B W I E J A B Z D R
S E A A L O C K E C A R D A N Q F T H
P T E B H F O K P L O S K I N T S M C
F I R X V F O X Q B J N E O L L B K N
X T T D Z A E R I W A U I B N A T P A
C I N D U M A N K H Y M H N A P Q Z R
R V O G N E S M Y C Y Y C T E L I F B
T E M U V O D Q H L J B N Q E P L R B
S I E Q N H P A S A D E N A P M G W Q
```

## Word Bank

baseball

Branch Rickey

competitive

Dodgers

Hall of Fame

Hank Aaron

Jackie Robinson

Montreal Royals

New York

Pasadena

# Jackie Robinson Crossword

## Across

2. displaying a strong desire to win
4. the first year that Jackie was eligible, he was elected into this
7. a ball game played on a diamond shaped field
9. baseball player known for breaking the color barrier
10. president of the Brooklyn Dodgers

## Down

1. home state of the Brooklyn Dodgers
3. city in California where Jackie Robinson lived
5. top farm team of the Brooklyn Dodgers
6. baseball player who up until recently held the record for most home runs
8. major league team that Jackie Robinson primarily played for

# Timeline

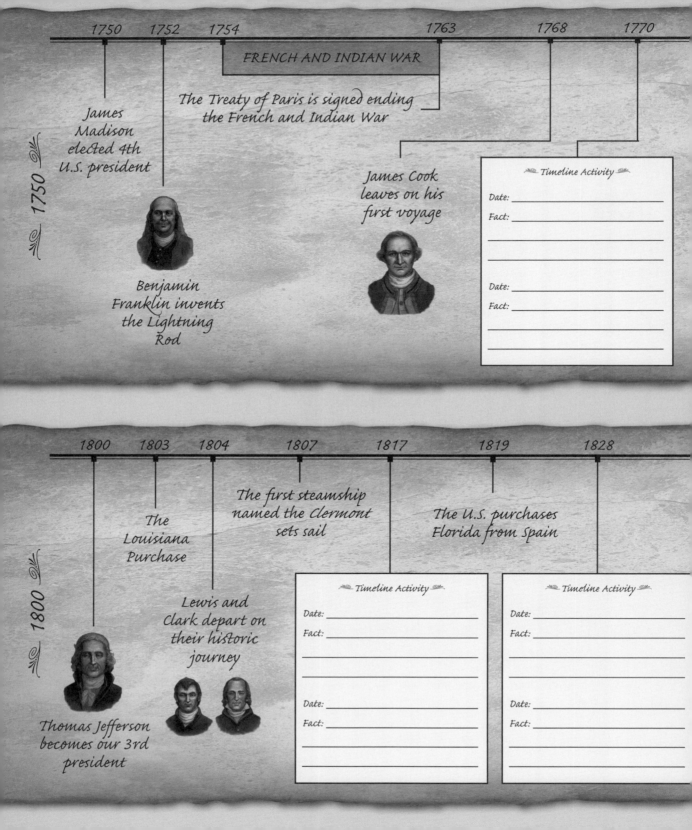

**1750**

1750 | 1752 | 1754 | 1763 | 1768 | 1770

FRENCH AND INDIAN WAR

The Treaty of Paris is signed ending the French and Indian War

James Madison elected 4th U.S. president

Benjamin Franklin invents the Lightning Rod

James Cook leaves on his first voyage

Timeline Activity

Date: _____
Fact: _____
_____
_____

Date: _____
Fact: _____
_____
_____

**1800**

1800 | 1803 | 1804 | 1807 | 1817 | 1819 | 1828

The Louisiana Purchase

The first steamship named the Clermont sets sail

The U.S. purchases Florida from Spain

Lewis and Clark depart on their historic journey

Thomas Jefferson becomes our 3rd president

Timeline Activity

Date: _____
Fact: _____
_____
_____

Date: _____
Fact: _____
_____
_____

Timeline Activity

Date: _____
Fact: _____
_____
_____

Date: _____
Fact: _____
_____
_____

**1775**

**1783**

**1789**

**1790**

THE REVOLUTIONARY WAR

Peace treaty with England
is signed that ends the
Revolutionary War

French
Revolution
begins

First census
taken in
America

Paul Revere's
Midnight Ride

### ❧ Timeline Activity ❧

Date: _____

Fact: _____

_____

_____

Date: _____

Fact: _____

_____

_____

### ❧ Timeline Activity ❧

Date: _____

Fact: _____

_____

_____

Date: _____

Fact: _____

_____

_____

*1800*

---

**1830**

**1832**

**1836**

**1844**

**1850**

**1852**

**1858**

First telegraph
sent by
Samuel Morse

Harriet
Tubman helps
her first group
of slaves to
freedom

Minnesota
becomes the
32nd state

Emily
Dickinson
is born

Abraham Lincoln
begins his political
career

### ❧ Timeline Activity ❧

Date: _____

Fact: _____

_____

_____

Date: _____

Fact: _____

_____

_____

### ❧ Timeline Activity ❧

Date: _____

Fact: _____

_____

_____

Date: _____

Fact: _____

_____

_____

*1860*

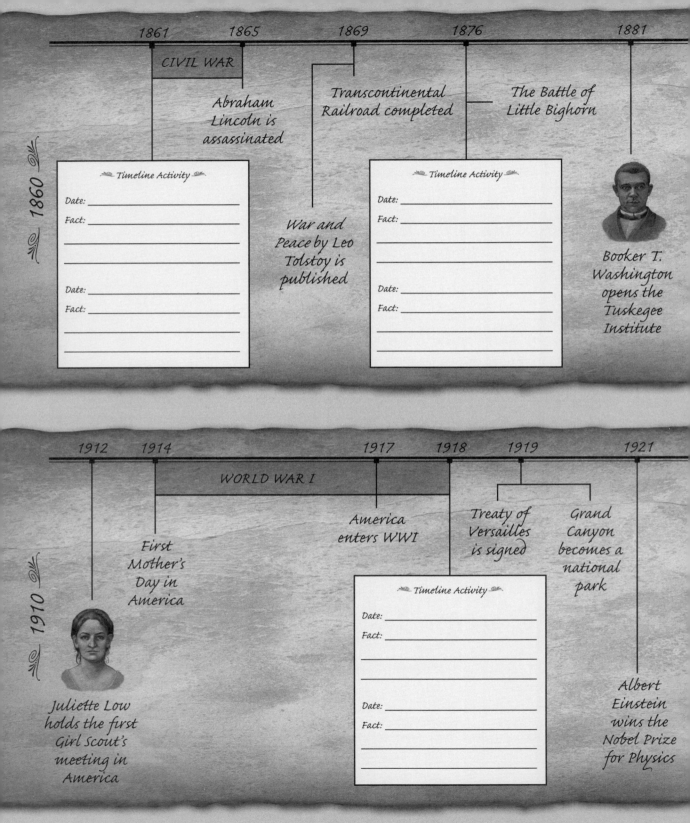

**1860**

1861     1865     1869     1876     1881

CIVIL WAR

Abraham Lincoln is assassinated

Transcontinental Railroad completed

The Battle of Little Bighorn

War and Peace by Leo Tolstoy is published

Booker T. Washington opens the Tuskegee Institute

≈ Timeline Activity ≈

Date: _____

Fact: _____

_____

_____

Date: _____

Fact: _____

_____

_____

≈ Timeline Activity ≈

Date: _____

Fact: _____

_____

_____

_____

Date: _____

Fact: _____

_____

_____

**1910**

1912   1914     1917   1918   1919     1921

WORLD WAR I

First Mother's Day in America

America enters WWI

Treaty of Versailles is signed

Grand Canyon becomes a national park

Juliette Low holds the first Girl Scout's meeting in America

Albert Einstein wins the Nobel Prize for Physics

≈ Timeline Activity ≈

Date: _____

Fact: _____

_____

_____

Date: _____

Fact: _____

_____

_____

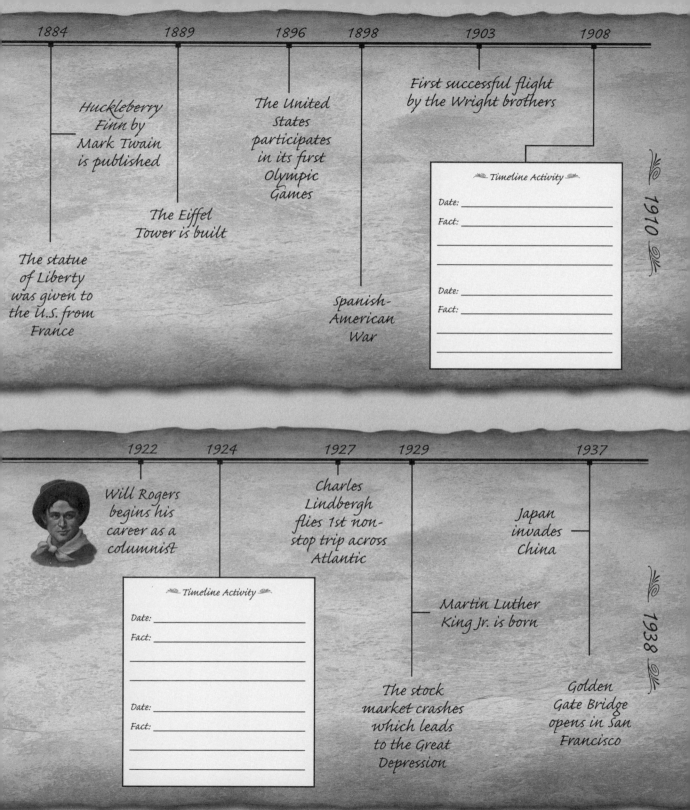

**1884** — The statue of Liberty was given to the U.S. from France

**1889** — Huckleberry Finn by Mark Twain is published / The Eiffel Tower is built

**1896** — The United States participates in its first Olympic Games

**1898** — Spanish-American War

**1903** — First successful flight by the Wright brothers

**1908** —

**1910**

*Timeline Activity*

Date: _____

Fact: _____

_____

_____

Date: _____

Fact: _____

_____

**1922** — Will Rogers begins his career as a columnist

**1924**

**1927** — Charles Lindbergh flies 1st non-stop trip across Atlantic

**1929** — Martin Luther King Jr. is born / The stock market crashes which leads to the Great Depression

**1937** — Japan invades China / Golden Gate Bridge opens in San Francisco

**1938**

*Timeline Activity*

Date: _____

Fact: _____

_____

_____

Date: _____

Fact: _____

_____

**1939**  **1940**  **1941**

WORLD WAR II

Germany invades Poland
Beginning WWII

Pearl Harbor is attacked    America enters
by the Japanese             World War II

**1938**

### ❧ Timeline Activity ❧

Date: _____

Fact: _____

_____

_____

Date: _____

Fact: _____

_____

_____

### ❧ Timeline Activity ❧

Date: _____

Fact: _____

_____

_____

Date: _____

Fact: _____

_____

_____

### ❧ Timeline Activity ❧

Date: _____

Fact: _____

_____

_____

Date: _____

Fact: _____

_____

_____

---

**1947**   **1950**   **1952**   **1953**   **1954**

KOREAN WAR

Dwight D.
Eisenhower
becomes our 34th
president

Racial segregation
in schools
is declared
unconstitutional

**1946**

### ❧ Timeline Activity ❧

Date: _____

Fact: _____

_____

_____

Date: _____

Fact: _____

_____

_____

**1942** | **1944** | **1945**

1946

Japan surrenders
ending WWII

### Timeline Activity

Date: _____

Fact: _____

_____

_____

Date: _____

Fact: _____

_____

_____

### Timeline Activity

Date: _____

Fact: _____

_____

_____

Date: _____

Fact: _____

_____

_____

Allied forces
invade North
Africa

V-E Day
occurs on
May 8th

---

**1958** | **1959** | **1960** | **1961** | **1963**

1966

NASA is
formed

Civil Rights
movement
begins

Martin Luther
King Jr. gives his
famous "I Have
a Dream" speech

First
American
satellite is
launched

The first
American
astronaut
travels into
space

Alaska and
Hawaii become
the 49th and 50th
states

President John
F. Kennedy is
assassinated

**Amos Fortune**
Purchases his freedom 1770

**George Washington**
Becomes our 1st president 1789

**Alexander Hamilton**
1st Secretary of the Treasury 1789

**Thomas Hopkins Gallaudet**
Opens 1st school for the Deaf 1817

**Noah Webster**
Dictionary published 1828

**William McGuffey**
*McGuffey Readers* published 1836

**Harriet Beecher Stowe**
*Uncle Tom's Cabin* published 1852

**Abraham Lincoln**
Becomes our 16th president 1861

**Alexander Graham Bell**
1st clear words on telephone 1876

Henry Ford
Model T revolutionizes travel 1908

Alvin C. York
Defeats a battalion 1918

Hellen Keller
Joins the A.F.B. 1924

Irena Sendler
Assists Jews in Warsaw Ghetto 1939

Winston Churchill
Prime Minister of England 1940

Dr. Charles Drew
Thesis on "Banked Blood" 1940

Dwight D. Eisenhower
Allied forces invade Normandy 1944

Corrie ten Boom
Released from Ravensbruck 1944

Jackie Robinson
Breaks the color barrier 1947

# Answer Key

## Amos Fortune

**Wordscramble:**

1. Africa
2. Violet Baldwin
3. Ichabod Richardson
4. tanner
5. Woburn
6. Amos Fortune
7. Jaffrey
8. epitaph
9. Elizabeth Yates
10. freedom

## George Washington

**Wordscramble:**

1. Mount Vernon
2. commander in chief
3. Continental Army
4. Revolutionary War
5. ragtag army
6. Martha Washington
7. president
8. Cabinet
9. George Washington
10. farewell address

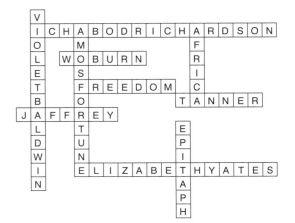

# Alexander Hamilton

## Wordscramble:

1. Revolutionary War
2. Treasury
3. King's College
4. St. Croix
5. New York
6. George Washington
7. Federalist Papers
8. economics
9. charisma
10. Alexander Hamilton

# Thomas Hopkins Gallaudet

## Wordscramble:

1. sign language
2. purpose
3. Alice Cogswell
4. Thomas Hopkins Gallaudet
5. deaf
6. Laurent Clerc
7. Sophia Fowler
8. Hartford
9. revolutionary
10. principal

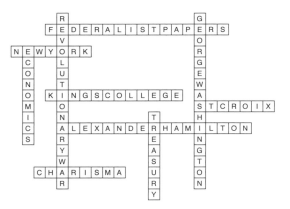

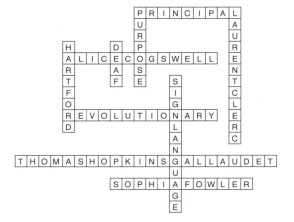

# Noah Webster

**Wordscramble:**

1. Yale
2. teacher
3. Noah Webster
4. lexicographer
5. dictionary
6. Hartford
7. speller
8. Rebecca Greenleaf
9. textbook
10. perseverance

# William McGuffey

**Wordscramble:**

1. Harriet Spining
2. Ohio
3. William McGuffey
4. *McGuffey Readers*
5. morals
6. professor
7. University
8. textbook
9. minister
10. schoolmaster

# Harriet Beecher Stowe

**Wordscramble:**

1. Hartford
2. Fugitive Slave Act
3. *Uncle Tom's Cabin*
4. vision
5. National Era
6. Civil War
7. Abraham Lincoln
8. Harriet Beecher Stowe
9. faith
10. author

# Abraham Lincoln

**Wordscramble:**

1. Civil War
2. Gettysburg Address
3. president
4. Emancipation Proclamation
5. Abraham Lincoln
6. speech
7. Mount Rushmore
8. liberator
9. Great Emancipator
10. Lincoln Memorial

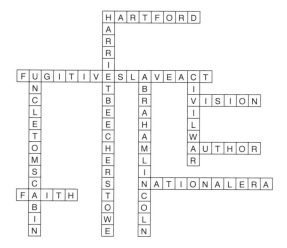

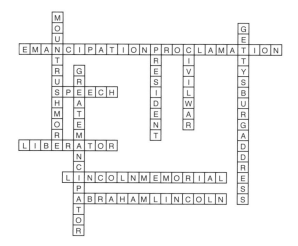

## Alexander Graham Bell

**Wordscramble:**

1. Scotland
2. harmonic telegraph
3. Mabel Hubbard
4. Boston
5. Thomas Watson
6. telephone
7. Alexander Graham Bell
8. microphone
9. loud speaker
10. inventor

## Henry Ford

**Wordscramble:**

1. invention
2. Henry Ford
3. Ford Motor Company
4. Thomas Edison
5. innovation
6. assembly line
7. Model T
8. pioneer
9. gas car
10. Michigan

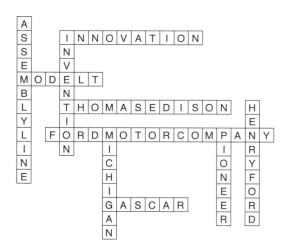

## *Alvin C. York*

**Wordscramble:**

1. sergeant
2. Pall Mall
3. World War I
4. Camp Gordon
5. Gracie Williams
6. Argonne Forest
7. France
8. Medal of Honor
9. Alvin C. York
10. marksman

## *Helen Keller*

**Wordscramble:**

1. Braille
2. Hellen Keller
3. lip reading
4. Perkins Institution
5. mute
6. cum laude
7. Radcliffe College
8. Vaudeville
9. Tuscumbia
10. Anne Sullivan

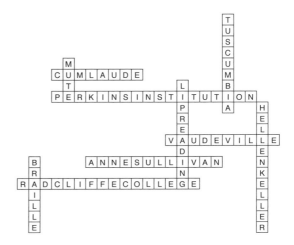

## Irena Sendler

**Wordscramble:**

1. Poland
2. Warsaw Ghetto
3. Zegota
4. Pawaik Prison
5. bribe
6. Irena Sendler
7. social worker
8. Holocaust
9. Kansas
10. courageous

## Winston Churchill

**Wordscramble:**

1. Boer War
2. Sandhurst
3. Clementine Hozier
4. World War II
5. Adolf Hitler
6. England
7. Prime Minister
8. House of Commons
9. Winston Churchill
10. orator

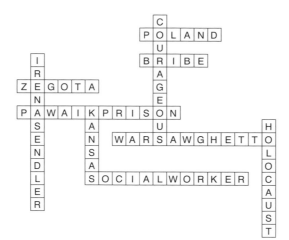

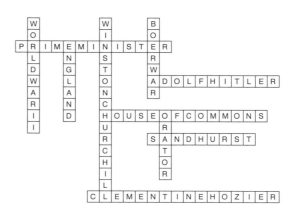

# Dr. Charles Drew

**Wordscramble:**

1. athlete
2. preservation
3. Washington D.C.
4. Red Cross
5. plasma
6. Dr. Charles Drew
7. transfusion
8. doctor
9. Columbia University
10. blood bank

# Dwight D. Eisenhower

**Wordscramble:**

1. West Point
2. Dwight D. Eisenhower
3. Axis
4. Allied Army
5. Mamie Doud
6. Big Three
7. Operation Overlord
8. World War II
9. invasion
10. Five Star General

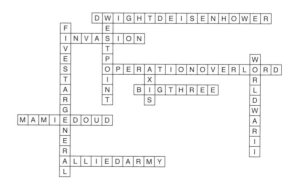

# Corrie ten Boom

**Wordscramble:**

1. Betsie
2. Ravensbruck
3. watchmaker
4. Dutch
5. forgiveness
6. concentration camp
7. Haarlem
8. Corrie ten Boom
9. hiding place
10. Gestapo

# Jackie Robinson

**Wordscramble:**

1. Montreal Royals
2. Jackie Robinson
3. Pasadena
4. competitive
5. baseball
6. Dodgers
7. New York
8. Hall of Fame
9. Branch Rickey
10. Hank Aaron

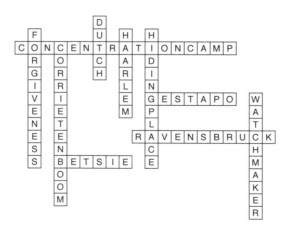

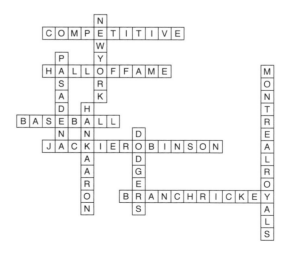

# Activity Samples

## Sample True or False:

Decide whether the following statements are true or false.

1. _____ George Washington preferred to be called "majesty" during his presidency.

2. _____ The people of America elected Washington as leader of the Continental Army.

3. _____ George Washington was born at the Mount Vernon estate.

4. _____ The Army of Great Britain far outnumbered the American Army.

5. _____ George Washington was never injured in a battle.

Answers:

1. F          2. F          3. F          4. T          5. T

## Sample Obituary

Mount Vernon, Virginia—America's first President died of a severe throat infection on the night of December 14th, 1799, at the age of 67. Greatly loved by the country, he led America in war and peace. President Washington set the standard for outstanding leadership in America.

## Trail Guide to Geography Series -
by Cindy Wiggers

Three books in the *Trail Guide to ...Geography* series include U.S., World, and Bible geography. Each book provides clear directions and assignment choices to encourage self-directed learning as students create their own personal geography notebooks. Daily atlas drills, mapping activities, and various weekly assignment choices address learning styles in a way that has kids asking for more! Use each book over several years by choosing more difficult activities as students grow older.

### Trail Guide features:
- Weekly lesson plans – for 36 weeks
- 5-minute daily atlas drills (2 questions/day, four days/week)
- 3 levels of difficulty – all ages participate together
- Weekly mapping assignments
- A variety of weekly research and hands-on activity choices

Student Notebooks are available on CD-ROM

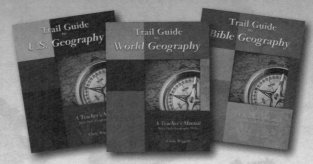

### Trail Guide Levels
The *Trail Guide* Levels are just a guide. Select a level according to student ability, and match level with the appropriate atlas or student notebook.

- Primary: grades 2–4
- Intermediate: grades 5–7
- Secondary: grades 8–12
All 3 levels in each book!

**Note:** Primary is ideal for independent 4th graders. Second and third graders will need plenty of guidance. If your oldest is 2nd–3rd grade range, please consider *Galloping the Globe* or *Cantering the Country* first.

## Trail Guide to U.S. Geography
Grades 2 - 12

"The *Trail Guide to U.S. Geography* provides lots of guidance while allowing for (and encouraging) flexibility and this is just the balance most homeschool moms need! The manual is easy to navigate and I am very impressed with how thoroughly material is covered. This resource is destined to be a favorite with homeschool families for years to come!"
–Cindy Prechtel, homeschoolingfromtheheart.com
Paperback, 144 pages, $18.95

## Trail Guide to World Geography
Grades 2 - 12

"We have the *Trail Guide to World Geography* and **love** it!! We are using it again this year just for the questions... I will never sell this guide!! I am looking forward to doing the U.S. one next year."
–Shannon, OK
Paperback, 128 pages, $18.95

## Trail Guide to Bible Geography
Grades 2 - 12

"Here is another winner from Geography Matters! *Trail Guide to Bible Geography* is multi-faceted, user-friendly, and suited to a wide range of ages and abilities."
–Jean Hall, Eclectic Homeschool Association
Paperback, 128 pages, $18.95

## Galloping the Globe
by Loreé Pettit and Dari Mullins
Grades K - 4

"If you've got kindergarten through fourth grade students, and are looking for unit study material for geography, hold on to your hat and get ready for *Galloping the Globe!* Loreé Pettit and Dari Mullins have written this great resource to introduce children to the continents and some of their countries. This book is designed to be completed in one to three years, depending on how much time you spend on each topic. And for each continent, there are suggestions and topics galore." –Leslie Wyatt, www.homeschoolenrichment.com

Organized by continent, incorporates student notebooking, and covers these topics:
- Basic Geography
- History & Biographies
- Literature
- Science
- Bible
- Activities
- Internet Sources
- Language Arts

This new 2010 edition of *Galloping the Globe* includes an Activity CD-ROM jam-packed with all the reproducible activity sheets found in the book plus added bonus pages. Paperback with CD-ROM, 272 pages, $29.95

## Cantering the Country
by Loreé Pettit and Dari Mullins
Grades 1–5

Saddle up your horses and strap on your thinking caps. Learning geography is an adventure. From the authors who brought you *Galloping the Globe,* you'll love its U.S. counterpart, *Cantering the Country.* This unit study teaches a wide range of academic and spiritual disciplines using the geography of the U.S. as a starting point. With this course, you won't have to put aside one subject to make time for another. They're all connected! This comprehensive unit study takes up to three years to complete and includes all subjects except math and spelling. Incorporates student notebooking and covers these topics:

- U.S. Geography
- Character
- Science
- Language Arts
- Activities
- Literature
- Civics
- History & Biographies & More

In addition to the 250+ page book, you will receive a CD-ROM packed full of reproducible outline maps and activities. Dust off your atlas and get ready to explore America! Paperback with CD-ROM, 272 pages, $29.95

## Adventures of Munford Series
### by Jamie Aramini

Although he's just two parts hydrogen and one part oxygen, Munford is all adventure. He can be rain, snow, sleet, or steam. He has traveled the world in search of excitement. Throughout history, he has been present at some of the most important and world-changing events. Fun and educational, Munford will inspire your children to learn more about many of history's greatest events. These readers make a great addition to your learning experience in areas such as history, geography, and science. This book series was written on an elementary reading level, but provides plenty of read-aloud entertainment for the entire family! Paperback, $8.95.

### The American Revolution

In this adventure, Munford travels to colonial America and experiences first hand the events leading to the American Revolution. He meets famed American Founding Fathers, such as Samuel Adams, Thomas Jefferson, and George Washington. He joins the Sons of Liberty under cover of night to dump tea into Boston Harbor. He tags along for Paul Revere's most famous ride, and even becomes a part of the Declaration of Independence in a way that you might not expect!

### The Klondike Gold Rush

In this adventure, Munford finds himself slap into the middle of the Klondike Gold Rush. He catches gold fever on this dangerous, yet thrilling, adventure. Meet some of the Gold Rush's most famous characters, like gold baron Alex McDonald or the tricky villain named Soapy Smith. Take a ride on the Whitehorse Rapids, and help Munford as he pans for gold. This is an adventure you won't soon forget!

### Munford Meets Robert Fulton

In this adventure, Munford meets a young boy in colonial America with a knack for inventing. The boy grows up to become one of the world's leading inventors, Robert Fulton! Join Munford and Fulton as they race to create the world's first commercially successful steamboat. Along the way, you'll meet a colorful cast of characters, from Benjamin Franklin to Napoleon Bonaparte. Don't miss this exciting story as it takes you from a fledgling young nation, to the rivers of France, and back again!

### Munford Meets Lewis & Clark

In this adventure, join Munford on an epic adventure with Meriwether Lewis and William Clark, as they make their perilous journey in search of the Northwest Passage to the Pacific Ocean.

## Eat Your Way Through the USA
### by Loreé Pettit

Taste your way around the U.S.A. without leaving your own dining room table! Each state has its unique geographical features, culinary specialities, and agricultural products. These influence both the ingredients that go into a recipe and the way food is prepared. Compliment your geography lesson and tantalize your tastebuds at the same time with this outstanding cookbook.

This cookbook includes a full meal of easy to follow recipes from each state. Recipes are easy to follow. Though they aren't written at a child's level, it's easy to include your students in the preparation of these dishes. Cooking together provides life skills and is a source of bonding and pride. More than just a cookbook, it is a taste buds-on approach to geography. Spiral bound, 118 pages, $14.95

## Eat Your Way Around the World
### by Jamie Aramini

Get out the sombrero for your Mexican fiesta! Chinese egg rolls... corn pancakes from Venezuela...fried plantains from Nigeria. All this, and more, is yours when you take your family on a whirlwind tour of over thirty countries in this unique international cookbook. Includes a full meal of recipes from each country. Recipes are easy to follow, and ingredients are readily available. Jam-packed with delicious dinners, divine drinks, and delectable desserts, this book is sure to please.

The entire family will be fascinated with tidbits of culture provided for each country including: Etiquette hints, Food Profiles, and Culture a la Carte. For more zest, add an activity and violà, create a memorable learning experience that will last for years to come. Some activities include: Food Journal, Passport, and World Travel Night. Spiral bound, 120 pages, $14.95

## Geography Through Art
### by Sharon Jeffus and Jamie Aramini

*Geography Through Art* is the ultimate book of international art projects. Join your children on an artistic journey to more than twenty-five countries spanning six continents (includes over a dozen United States projects). Previously published by Visual Manna as *Teaching Geography Through Art*, Geography Matters has added a number of enhancements and practical changes to this fascinating art book. Use this book as an exciting way to supplement any study of geography, history, or social studies. You'll find yourself reaching for this indispensable guide again and again to delight and engage students in learning about geography through the culture and art of peoples around the world. Paperback, 190 pages, $19.95

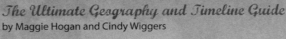

## The Ultimate Geography and Timeline Guide

by Maggie Hogan and Cindy Wiggers

Grades K - 12

Learn how to construct timelines, establish student notebooks, teach geography through literature, and integrate science with activities on volcanoes, archaeology, and other subjects. Use the complete multi-level geography course for middle and high school students. Now includes CD-ROM of all reproducible activity and planning pages. Use for all students kindergarden through high school. Paperback with CD-ROM, 353 pages, $39.95

- 18 Reproducible Outline Maps
- Teaching Tips
- Planning Charts
- Over 150 Reproducible Pages
- Over 300 Timeline Figures
- Lesson Plans
- Scope and Sequence
- Flash Cards
- Games

## Mark-It Timeline of History

There's hardly no better way to keep history in perspective than creating a timeline in tandem with your history studies. This poster is just the tool to do so. Write or draw images of events as they are studied, or attach timeline figures to aid student understanding and comprehension of the topic at hand. 23" x 34". Laminated, $10.95, Paper (folded), $5.95

## Profiles from History Series

by Ashley (Strayer) Wiggers

Looking for a way to help your students connect with history? The *Profiles from History* series is dedicated to telling the stories of people, whose lives are worth remembering. Whether they made a discovery, led heroically in a war, created a masterpiece through music, or art, used a pen to change the world, or impacted humanity with their bravery, they made a difference. We can learn so much by looking at those who came before us. Be ready to change your mind about history, with *Profiles from History*, Volumes 1, 2, & 3. Paperback, $16.95

## - Reproducible Outline Maps -

Reproducible outline maps have a myriad of uses in the home, school, and office. Uncle Josh's quality digital maps provide opportunities for creative learning at all ages. His maps feature rivers and grid lines where possible, and countries are shown in context with their surroundings. (No map of Germany "floating" in the center of the page, here!) When students use outline maps and see the places they are studying in context when they gain a deeper understanding of the subject at hand.

## Uncle Josh's Outline Map Book

Take advantage of those spontaneous teaching moments when you have this set of outline maps handy. They are:

- Over 100 reproducible maps
- 15 world regions
- Continents with and without borders
- 25 countries
- Each of the 50 United States
- 8 U.S. regions

Useful for all grades and topics, this is by far one of the best book of reproducible outline maps you'll find. Paperback, 128 pages, $19.95

## Uncle Josh's Outline Map Collection CD-ROM

In addition to all maps in *Uncle Josh's Outline Map Book* the CD-Rom includes color, shaded-relief, and labeled maps. Over 260 printable maps plus bonus activities. CD-ROM (Mac & Windows), $26.95

## - Large-scale Maps -

Large-scale maps are great for detail labeling and for family or classroom use. Laminated Mark-It maps can be reused for a variety of lessons. Quality digital map art is used for each of the fifteen map titles published and laminated by Geography Matters. Choose from large scale continents, regions, United States, and world maps. US and World available in both outline version and with state, country, and capitals labeled. Ask about our ever expanding library of full, color shaded-relief maps. Paper and laminated, each title available separately or in discounted sets.

# TRAIL GUIDE TO LEARNING

Introducing... ***The Trail Guide to Learning series***, an innovative new curriculum from Geography Matters. This series provides all the guidance and materials necessary to teach your children the way you've always wanted—effectively, efficiently, and enjoyably. But most of all, *Trail Guide to Learning* equips you to achieve the foremost objective of a homeschooling program—developing and nurturing relationships with your children! The tutoring approach makes each lesson individual, yet flexible enough to meet the needs of several grades at once. The sourcebook provides the instruction, clearly laid out in daily sections that make lesson planning a breeze. Just add in the necessary resources for success, available in our money-saving packages, and you'll have a curriculum for multiple grade levels that will last all year and cover every subject but math!

| *Paths of Exploration* | *Paths of Settlement* | *Paths of Progress* |
|---|---|---|
| **Grades 3-5** | **Grades 4-6** | **Grades 5-7** |

*Paths of Exploration* is the first step on the *Trail Guide to Learning*. It takes students on a journey. Follow the steps of famous explorers and pioneers across America and let geography be your guide to science, history, language skills, and the arts. This journey will teach students HOW to think by asking, answering, and investigating questions about our great country's beginning and growth. The paths of the explorers are seen through multi-disciplinary eyes, but always with the same goals: to make learning enjoyable, memorable, and motivating. This full one-year course is targeted for grades 3-5, but the lessons can be easily adapted for 2nd and 6th grades as well.

*Paths of Settlement* is the second step on the *Trail Guide to Learning*. Key events studied include the Colonial Period, the Revolutionary War, the war of 1812, the Civil War, and Westward Expansion. Learn about the accomplishments of great Americans such as George Washington and Patrick Henry who built upon the trial blazed by brave explorers. Their actions teach us the principles of freedom and citizenship - founding and expanding our country, strengthening us in times of war and binding us together in times of struggle. This full one-year course is targeted for grades 4-6, but the lessons can be easily adapted for 3rd and 7th grades as well.

*Paths of Progress* is the third step on the *Trail Guide to Learning*. To grow as a country, another group of leaders had to step forward during our history—scientists and inventors. Study those who used their talents and abilities to answer questions that provided better ways of living and working. The lives of these devoted individuals and their contributions will be examined throughout our history, into the Industrial Revolution and the beginning of the 20th century. Primary science focus involves Physical Science and the economic impact of each development. This full one-year course is targeted for grades 5-7, but the lessons can easily be adapted for 4th and 8th grades as well.

**Look online now for more information and to view sample pages.**

**www.TrailGuidetoLearning.com** • **800-426-4650**

# About the Author

Ashley (Strayer) Wiggers grew up in the early days of the home schooling movement taught by parents, Greg and Debbie Strayer, who are authors of numerous home schooling materials. A home school graduate, Ashley enjoyed a 10-year career as a national champion synchronized swimmer and is currently the head coach of the Pulaski County High School swim team. Ashley speaks at home school seminars across the country, edits a monthly online newsletter for Geography Matters, and is the author of the *Profiles from History* series.

Ashley makes her home in Somerset, KY, with her husband, Alex, and can't wait to someday continue the home school philosophies and ideals that her parents and in-laws have passed on with her own children.